Money Does Grow On Trees

15 Books To Transform Your Wealth Mindset

John Bolton

Money Does Grow On Trees
ISBN: 978-0-6454830-1-7

First published in Great Britain
in 2022 through Amazon self-publishing
service Kindle Direct Publishing

Disclaimer: The disclaimer is to say only some of the names and places have been changed.

Produced by samanthahoughton.co.uk

Contents

Acknowledgements and Thanks

Thanks to the 16 Authors for the exceptional 15 titles that I have summarized in this book. My hope for you, the reader, after reading my summaries, is for you to purchase and read the original books.

Also, I would hope that the authors would be happy with my summary of their books. Half of the authors have passed on since writing their work, so I am also talking to their wives, sons, daughters and any relatives who are associated with them. Some of these books have become more difficult to obtain as hard copies. Hopefully, there will be enough renewed interest for their publishers to reprint.

There are no words to describe my thanks (and gratefulness) to my wife Tricia for her support in this undertaking and my life in general. Life is so much easier when you live with your soulmate.

Many thanks to Jim Fortin for firstly recommending some of these titles and then changing my life through his TCP program. We (my family) are living a better life having done this. Listen to his podcasts to see how he can help you.

Also, many thanks to Samantha Houghton for her assistance in editing and publishing this book. Having never done this before, Samantha has made the process easy and enjoyable. For any aspiring new writer, I would thoroughly recommend Sam to assist you with your endeavours.

10% of the proceeds of this book go to the Australian Food Bank, and a further 10% goes towards Feeding America (USA Food Bank).

Aims of This Book

I put this book together to help its readers to have a more enjoyable life by applying the concepts found in the 15 books I have explored. A better life can be achieved by improving your money consciousness and attracting more to you. It may be through improving your relationships with your loved ones or making it easier to get along with anyone. At the end of the day, what most of us truly want is purpose and happiness.

Also, I intend to improve the sales of the 15 books and spread awareness of the concepts that they bring. These books have changed many lives, but sometimes in our current world, the messages can be lost under the influence of social media and other distractions. Sometimes we need to slow down, appreciate what we have and learn something from a good book.

The giving plan gifted by the author is to help those of us who are struggling with life. Reading a book on improving your life would come secondary to finding food for yourself and your family for most people. Sometimes, all that is needed is some help.

Author Bio

John lives in Brisbane, Australia, with his wife Tricia and their three children. He is an Optometrist who owns his practice while running their personal superannuation fund and investing in real estate and the share market.

Helping and being of service to others are high values of John's and are the driving reason behind writing this book. Personal development is an important part of both John and Tricia's (life coach) life. Podcasts that he recommends are Lewis Howes (The School of Greatness), AlphaMind (Steven Goldstein and Mark Randal) and James Wedmore (Mind Your Business).

Having competed in several triathlons and half marathons, health and fitness are a passion and a means for keeping up with his kids. He is an avid "Survivor" fan (has previously applied) who loves watching sports and following his football teams (Miami Dolphins and Brisbane Broncos).

John loves people and hopes this book will help others gain awareness and learn how they have the power to create a new financial future for themselves and their loved ones. You don't have to be a financial mogul to succeed - you can be an everyday person going to work and still attain the success you want. It is possible.

Introduction

This is not a "normal money" book. This book introduces 15 other books that can change your life in so many ways. These books will help you grow financially and spiritually and generally lead to having more happiness in your life. The knowledge gained is priceless if you apply it to your world.

Does money grow on trees? Technically, no; however, money or success at whatever you do is obtainable for anyone that desires it. The chances of being wealthy are infinite in our world. And the best thing about all of this is that the answers many are looking for can be found by looking in a mirror. We all have potential and our strengths - it is just a matter of knowing how to convert our potential.

From a personal point of view, my life changed significantly in 2019, having gone through my personal development transformation. This change came from participating in Jim Fortins' TCP program and reading these books. I read some of these books in my 30s, but I needed to re-read them to understand and use the concepts thoroughly.

Life for us at this stage was "comfortable", but life after this was much better in so many different ways. Personal relationships became easier, I wasn't as affected by the external as much, and there was more joy in our lives. My business sales went up by 30-40% by changing my thoughts and outlook on life.

So, when Covid happened in early 2020, it had little or no effect on my business as I only focused on the internal, not the craziness of the external world at the time. My business flourished while seeing fewer clients than before, and other shops closed around me. At the same time, I renegotiated my new lease at a lower rent than previously, compared to previous "negotiations", which always increased. This concept is not rocket science.

Some of the titles here are best sellers and very well known; some are not. To the millennial readers, you will be at a great advantage to learn the concepts earlier than I and many others have. I was 55 by the time I had done this, and one regret (if you can call it that) is that it would have been a huge advantage to read them by the age of 25. However, you are never too old for any of this. Learning is one of the true joys of life—also the benefits of this knowledge.

The concepts discussed here have been around for hundreds or thousands of years. Only 3 of these titles were written in the 21st century, but don't let that mean anything. Many of today's titles about the same topics found their inspiration from these books.

We live in a somewhat crazy world, where we are told by society and by our (well-meaning) parents that getting an education and working hard is the way to success and happiness. A college or university education seems to be the logical move for many of us, but many don't need to do this.

Before you question this, ask yourself how many truly wealthy people in society have a university or higher education degree or more. The answer is - not many.

We are "pressured" by society to work hard and study hard to get further ahead, but what if the true answer to success is nothing to do with this. There is also a rush to get "out there" and start earning money through a job, with little or no regard for how to really save and invest our earnings. More time needs to be spent on this topic rather than studying something else that you won't use in your lifetime. The concepts in these books will open and expand your mind as you read them. You will find yourself questioning many of the things that you regarded as the truth – when in actual fact, they are just learned beliefs by the conditioning we receive in life. There is a huge difference. Most of the things that we hold dear to ourselves are learned beliefs. You have to ask yourself, "What do I gain by having that belief?" If the answer is not much, then you alone have the choice to change your life.

The 15 titles you are about to dive into are like a map containing the necessary tools to change your life. My book gives you a small taste of what these books offer, and if you feel aligned with the feel/message of the book, go ahead and buy it.

Only by buying and embracing these books will you understand their full concept. Sometimes the best thing you can do is give yourself some peaceful time by staying out of the monkey chatter of the world, sitting down and reading a good book.

Enjoy!

CHAPTER ONE

Think and Grow Rich (Napoleon Hill) 1937

Andrew Carnegie inspired Napoleon Hill to study the successes of more than 500 exceedingly wealthy men. This process took over 20 years to complete. Carnegie was convinced that much of what is taught in schools has no value in wealth creation or earning a living. It would be interesting if he would have a different opinion now, more than 100 years later, about the effectiveness of our school systems. I very much doubt it.

Carnegie's secret of wealth creation was passed to virtually every who's who of American businessmen of the late 1800s and early 1900s. This book is the first of its kind to put together the ideas and methods of such a distinguished group. Even though this book isn't the first self-improvement book, it is by far the most influential of its era and for the next 100 years or so. Sales of this book are reported to be more than 40 million. Most people in the self-development field today recognise the influence of this book.

This book aims to provide the reader with the 'how-to' in creating their wealth. Napoleon Hill outlines 13 steps to reach goals in life. In the introduction, he talks of 3 main qualities – desire, persistence and determination. These traits are a common theme throughout the whole of this book. Modern day examples of people who succeeded with these traits are Steve Jobs (Apple) and Colonel Sanders (KFC). Their paths were not easy, and there were plenty of obstacles in their way. The lesson here is to keep pushing regardless of how hard things become, and success will come. One of "mankind's" problems is that we know what doesn't "work" as we believe that our limitations are real. The reality is that these are just our thoughts, nothing more and certainly nothing real. Instead, we should condition our minds with the desire for success and wealth.

Step 1 is Desire

This is where our dreams and aspirations are formed. Desire is definite, whereas hope and wishing are not. We must see ourselves as the successful person that we desire to be. This way, it is either successful or not; there is no backtracking. There are stories of adventurers like Cortez who had his ships burned when they reached the Americas, so there was no turning back to the "safety" of home. This way, his men had to "make it work" for their futures. There are six basic steps to translating the desire for success into reality. When you buy the book, you can read about them on page 26. Those who can see themselves as rich and successful in the future have a strong chance of success. Those of us who cannot see this probably won't succeed.

In your imagination, great riches need to be plentiful. The world is constantly changing, and there are opportunities for all of us. The "practical dreamers" of the world are the ones that make a difference for everyone. Examples of this are Lincoln, Ford, Edison and Marconi. People who believed in the "impossible" achieved it anyway. Success didn't come easy to these people; however, they DID NOT QUIT. You may say that's because they were intelligent, able, and had easy opportunities for them. If so, then what about people like Helen Keller (who was deaf, dumb and blind) or Steven Hawking, who was confined to his wheelchair and could only talk with the assistance of a computer. Our thoughts can be both our limitations and our reason for success. We need to believe in ourselves and what we want to achieve and keep an open mind for our path toward success. Read the inspiring story about the author and his son on page 37 and believe that anyone can have success and joy in their lives.

Don't let the environment or others (even so-called experts) change your thoughts or opinions. Also, realise that you will always find negative people towards new ideas or inventions. Believe in the power of your desire and your faith, and believe in yourself. Remember, the universe (or nature) doesn't understand the word impossible - so why should you?

Step 2 is Faith

Faith is the key to obtaining what we desire. Our subconscious works optimally when our positive emotions are stimulated. Our most positive emotions are faith, love and sex. Faith is created by affirmations repeated to our subconscious - this is auto-suggestion. Repetition is paramount as the more we keep telling ourselves something, the more we will believe it to be the truth. The more emotive the impulse of our thoughts, the stronger the belief will become. It is a bit like training your subconscious. While it works well with our positive emotions, it also works negatively with our negative emotions. The use of negative emotions leads to the belief of one being doomed to a life of lack and failure. Have you ever noticed the difference between a cancer patient with a positive outlook and a negative outlook? One viewpoint focuses on having an opportunity to survive longer, while the other gives up. Our subconscious can easily pick up positive or negative emotions. It is obvious which one we need to use, but this is our choice and nobody else's.

Having faith in positivity, abundance, infinite wealth, and ourselves is the way to a successful life. Using our positive emotions with faith, we become like magnets to all things positive. The fear of disease, failure, and poverty attracts negatives into our environment. We are what we are due to the vibrations of our thoughts either way. Read the self-confidence formula on page 58 to make understanding this easier. Regularly doing this, you will become more self-reliant, and success will follow. An important note is that our subconscious doesn't differentiate between positive or destructive thoughts, so being aware of our thoughts here is crucial. If we are full of fear (for whatever reason), then this will translate to a life of disappointment and lack.

Love and faith work hand in hand. Together they work to create a positive field of magnetic attraction, which strengthens our achievements in life. Gandhi and Jesus are two powerful examples of this where faith has conquered what would have seemed to be impossible. Think of people you just love being around, and you will see day-to-day examples of this.

The principles of faith and co-operation are essential to business; giving more to the employers first before flowing out to the employees. People will follow leaders who have the same principles as Gandhi. There is a very interesting story about big business, faith and desire on page 67 that is well worth reading. This story demonstrates how desire can be translated into physical achievement. Our thoughts determine our levels of wealth, as there are no limits to what our minds can achieve. The only limits to this are those that we place on ourselves. Consider the modern day tech giants who mostly were not even a thought 20 years ago.

Step 3 Auto-Suggestion

Auto-suggestion is how we influence the subconscious mind and, as such, is probably the most influential chapter of this book. All thoughts need to have auto-suggestions to reach our subconscious, and this is where we need to control the passage. If we neglect this control, then we await a life of less and more misery. Our suggestions must have emotions or feelings. Without them, they will not be as effective as they don't influence the subconscious. As mentioned before, repetition is vital here as well.

Our ability to concentrate on our desires here also plays a large part in our success. We must be specific in what we want—for example, a certain amount of money, a new car, etc. Also, to picture in our minds what this desire looks like and saying things out loud with feeling is part of this. Having absolute faith in our desires increases our ability to direct our subconscious - we have to believe in our future success. As with all of the steps here, practice makes perfect.

Step 4 Specialized Knowledge

Good general knowledge is never enough to attract money, whereas applied knowledge will lead to riches. It's like reading this book and loving it before stacking it on your favourite shelf (or adding it to your Kindle collection). It will remain a nice informative read without doing the exercises and implementing what this book tells you. THIS KNOWLEDGE HAS TO BE APPLIED. Riches don't just come from osmosis.

Andrew Carnegie, who made his fortune as a steel magnate, didn't have the knowledge about steel that many others had. So he surrounded himself with others whose understanding was greater than his own.

Whatever field you go into, specialised knowledge is required. Acquiring this knowledge becomes easier if you do something that you have passion for and genuinely like doing. Any weakness can be less of a problem by having a Master Mind group behind you. This group can propel you to greater heights by giving advice, information or guidance when you best need it. Similar to having a mentor at your beck and call. Modern day life coaches can be part of this group.

Successful people keep acquiring specialised knowledge for the duration of their whole working lives. They probably keep doing so after they have finished, as it becomes a very powerful habit. This is perhaps part of why gifted academics are usually not the most successful. Being gifted can cause complacency as they find things to be "too easy" to do. The less gifted people, who are stronger in character and personality and keep learning, are far more successful. Anything that we achieve with little or no effort, we don't respect. We have to have skin in the game to realise our potential. It's like people who win the lottery and end up no better off financially in less than five years. We only respect what we have to pay for; free education is an example.

Think about what you want to do and what this looks like. An IDEA will form, and specialised knowledge will help that idea develop.

Step 5 Imagination

Most of our limitations in life come from our lack of imagination and desire. Our ability to imagine what could be is turned into what is, can be seen throughout the ages. Through our creative vision, we can communicate with infinite intelligence allowing us to "communicate" with the minds of others. The great achievers in history have been able to do this.

Think of the universe and yourself as just a bundle of energy. Thought impulses (imagination) are forms of energy. When you imagine with desire, you are attracting more of this energy. With the aid of nature, anything becomes possible (within reason), and ideas are just our starting point. The example of the enchanted kettle on page 115 is a good read. One of the biggest things to get here is that the only limitations are in our minds. The belief that only honest hard work will bring success and wealth is very limited. Money does not come from hard work alone.

In the book, the "new" field of opportunity was the radio and what this potentially could bring to anyone who took advantage of it. This was definitely true in the 1930s. In the 2020s, the internet and online businesses will be the equivalents. The example of Andrew Carnegie (steel magnate) with little knowledge of steel making shows that although knowledge is important, it isn't the be-all and end-all of everything. You can find knowledge. Suppose you are just waiting for a favourable break so that you can start your "project". You could be waiting a long time, or the favourable break will likely never happen. There is never a better time than now to achieve your dreams by making your breaks with imagination and determination.

Step 6 Organised Planning

This is the largest chapter in the book and has many very easy to follow steps, which I won't be repeating here.

The major key to planning is persistence. If your first plan doesn't work, try another until you find what works for you. A significant point of failure is giving up after the first plan didn't work and saying it was too hard. Most of the success stories of the last 2000 years or so involved some level of pain or initial defeat in the early stages. How many times did Edison attempt to invent the light bulb? Have you ever heard the story of Robert the Bruce, who drew inspiration from a spider weaving its web until it was done while failing many times? This inspired him to defeat the English armies.

Remember, a "quitter never wins, and a winner never quits" (p134).

In any organisation, there are leaders and followers. Leaders have to lead correctly; otherwise, the followers won't follow properly. Qualities of a leader include clarity, fairness, decisiveness, over-delivering and co-operation. Be the leader that others will want to follow, share profits and respect each other. Leaders who lead by force may have some success but rarely will this be sustained long term. The major causes of failure in leadership are on p140. Read this as it details what not to do. From p145-157, Hill talks about applying for a position and how to get the job that you want. Some of this information is outdated; however, the general theme is critical for those of us looking for a new path.

The success of marketing comes down to 3 essentials – quality, quantity and service. It is the same for employers and employees. One of the keys here is to over-deliver - give your client more than you promised. For marketing to work, this needs to become a habit.

On page 161, the 30 major causes of failure of people and businesses alike are listed. Some of these causes are environmental, but most come from an individual's mindset. Our thoughts can drive us to success or failure – we get to choose. As with anything in life, most of us can't see ourselves as others see us. We need to get to know ourselves better, and self-reflection helps here. On page 170, there are 28 questions to help with self-analysis. Once we better understand ourselves, we can learn to become more analytical and understand others also.

Interestingly, Hill talks about so-called leaders taking pot-shots at Wall Street, Big Business and Money Movers. Nothing has changed in almost one hundred years, and probably nothing will change in the next century. 'Take riches from the rich and give to the poor' will always be the mantra of those who don't accept any personal responsibility for where they are in life. The thought of "they must have done something illegal to get that much because there is no way I could have done that" is very common. In society, there are thoughts that "it is okay to do well, but just don't do too well, or we will try to bring you down." Unfortunately, this is part of human behaviour.

Many of us are consumed with the idea of more pay for less service or that the government should help us out. Thinking this way limits what you can do for yourself. In many "western" countries, we pride ourselves on living in a free country and having freedom. It is true to some extent, but we have to help ourselves, which requires some effort.

Einstein said, "for every action - there is an equal and opposite reaction." Nature/the universe doesn't allow something for nothing or receiving without giving. So when governments give us excesses without having the money, the reaction is that this money will have to be re-paid by future generations with interest.

Step 7 Decision

Lack of decision or procrastination is a major cause of failure for many of us. Personally, I know this from writing this book. The idea came years ago, but I did nothing about it until 2021, when I really started writing it. I had at least five years before that with the thought of "doing it later." Being in my comfort zone has much to do with this.

Many of us fail because others influence us, which moves us away from making decisions. Go with what feels right for you, reach your decision and take action. There will always be other people, some with good intentions and some not that will try to change your decision. Listen only to yourself or any mentors you have and trust and ignore the rest.

Great decisions come from great leaders who lead with courage. People such as Jesus, Joan of Arc, Lincoln, and Gandhi would have had many people around them "advising" them to take a different direction. What would they have achieved if they had listened to everybody? Unfortunately, these people paid the ultimate price for their courage. There is a great story of courage and decision making on page 194 about the events that led to the American declaration of independence in 1776. These decisions were likely made quickly, firmly and without reservation.

Indecision is a learnt habit. Regrettably, our school systems don't encourage quick, decisive decision making. This may be a reason why many of our great achievers spent less time in our education systems.

Step 8 Persistence

Persistence, when combined with desire, produces outcomes. Many of us give up when obstacles or misfortune appear. Successful people carry on regardless toward their goals. A lack of persistence is one of the primary causes of failure. Desire and imagination get us started, but it leads to very little without persistence.

Success tends to be drawn towards you once we have money consciousness (only positive thoughts of attracting money). It's like how a magnet attracts metal, which is increased by persistence.

On the other hand, poverty is attracted to people without money consciousness. So, without the persistence of changing that, the chances of lack or poverty increase. Persistence leads to success.

As with all of these qualities, habits strengthen them. If we make persistence a habit, then the chances of success increase significantly. Causes of persistence include desire, co-operation and a pattern of acting courageously. There are eight causes of persistence listed here compared to 16 causes of a lack of persistence. The lack list includes environmental reasons that we use to excuse failure. All eight causes of persistence are internal. Read the lists on Page 216.

One of the reasons for lack is the fear of criticism. Many abusive relationships have the abused person not leaving for fear of what other people will think. This fear prevents many of us from taking chances in life or correcting something not working in a relationship.

We have to make our own "breaks" to achieve success. The "breaks" don't just come to us; we have to be persistent with our goals to obtain them. Read the steps for the habit of persistence on page 222. Also, read the story of Mohammed on page 228, which is a great example of persistence and focused goals.

Step 9 Power of the Master Mind

Knowledge comes from infinite intelligence, our experiences and our use of creative imagination. Mentors or a group where advice and counsel work together to form great success can also be a source.

Energy is how nature works to build its creations. Our minds are a form of energy being spiritual. And when we co-ordinate with others, an affinity occurs, bringing our "mastermind" experience. Our brains are full of energy, a bit like a battery. When combined with other brains in harmony, it can create more energy than the sum of the individuals. Gandhi is an example of this. He attained his great power by inducing millions in the spirit of harmony for a specific goal.

Success comes from attraction, whereas failure comes from no planning and no attraction.

Step 10 The Mystery of Sex Transmutation

Sex transmutation is the transfer of sexual thought to thoughts that improve our imagination, courage, willpower, persistence and creative ability. It probably explains why men throughout the ages have run the risk of life and reputation to achieve this. Sex is the most powerful of all of our desires, and this is why men who have achieved great things in history have learnt the art of sex transmutation. It is also why these men were motivated by the influence of a woman (and vice versa).

Both are needed to achieve "great" things. Destroy the sex glands, and the primary source of action will be lost. The ten mind stimuli are listed on page 245, which greatly influence the mind.

A genius has been defined as a person who has discovered how to increase the vibration of thought that is not available through ordinary thought vibrations. They use their creative imagination with purpose.

When our brains are stimulated by one or multiple mind stimuli, exceptional thoughts become available. It is probably where the saying "behind every great man, there is a great woman" was born - and vice versa. And why greatness is present when they are together and lessens when they grow apart. People who have a "magnetic personality" owe this to their sex energy. Highly sexed people have plenty of magnetism, which can be communicated by just a handshake, tone, posture, personal appearance or vibrations of thought.

To be clear here, this isn't just about selling and can be used in all walks of life, whatever profession you are in. There is an element of "selling" to whatever you do. People who lack sex energy won't inspire or enthuse others to buy from them.

Like with everything in our lives, too much of one thing can be detrimental to us. Being highly sexed and using it intelligently can lead to success. However, too much emphasis on sex can destroy our reasoning and willpower, leading to possible mental disorders.

The emotions of love, romance and sex give us the ability to succeed to the degree that we allow for ourselves. Combining the three emotions can elevate us to the top of whatever mountain we wish to climb. Negative emotions cause the opposite effect. Be aware that our thoughts can change these emotions easily.

Sometimes it may be necessary to think of memories of love from the past to distract yourself from your present worries of life.

Step 11 The Subconscious Mind

An important chapter and one I think would have been substantially longer if written in the 21st century. Your subconscious works 24/7 and can be given any plan or idea to work with. Our subconscious works regardless of any effort to influence it or not. Our subconscious acts on our thoughts or desires mixed in with whatever emotional feelings we have with them. We must be clear with our aspirations.

Otherwise, the subconscious won't deliver the outcome that we want. Remember that the subconscious doesn't differentiate between positive and negative thoughts, so being clear and positive is essential here.

Our subconscious is very susceptible to thoughts with feelings or high emotions. Negative feelings can lead to many negative outcomes. The power of auto-suggestion helps positive feelings. Take note of the seven positive and seven negative emotions on page 278. Positive and negative emotions cannot coexist in the mind simultaneously. Develop a habit of using positive emotions, as a single negative thought can destroy all of the good. Remember that prayer with fear rarely produces a positive outcome.

Our subconscious is where our minds translate our thoughts into plans that we can use for a better life. Understanding this is crucial to where we want to go.

Step 12 The Brain

The brain receives and delivers all vibrations of thoughts that are around us. Through our emotions, particularly like sex, more vibrations can occur than without emotion. This, in turn, attracts ideas and thoughts from around us. Therefore, it is important to surround yourself with like-minded positive feeling people.

"Man", in general, understands very little of this concept. But this is where we can take advantage of our sixth sense. Using our brain, we need to use the subconscious mind, creative imagination and auto-suggestion - and all of this starts with desire.

Step 13 The Sixth Sense

The sixth sense is intangible, where things happen without using any of our five senses. It is a mixture of both mental and spiritual and comes from developing our minds through meditation. Light bulb moments or inspiration come from here. Having faith makes this easier to achieve. Meditation and self-hypnosis, along with our imagination, are the tools required.

We need to imagine ourselves doing and feeling what we want to achieve. The author uses an imaginary council where he asks for specific guidance on his goals. As with anything that we imagine, these meetings become almost real if we do it many times. The author becomes receptive to many ideas, thoughts, and knowledge. Hill used famous people for his council, which gave the council more authority.

Chapter 15 Ghosts of Fear

Indecision, doubt, and fear are the main negatives that prevent us from using our sixth sense. Fear is the main obstacle when it comes to controlling your life. The main fears are poverty, criticism, poor health, losing a loved one, getting older and death. Fear is just a state of mind. Understanding what you are fearful of helps with dealing with the fear. We all have fears, which we can control by controlling our minds.

Think of who you want to be, feel it and make a habit of doing this, and this will determine who you are. We do have a choice here.

The fear of poverty is probably the worst as it paralyses everything positive. Like all other fears, it is found in the mind; however, it is the hardest to overcome. Poverty brings a state of desperation and humility that can only be described by people who have experienced it. Symptoms include doubt, worry and procrastination. Money is at the root of this; our relationship with money, how we talk about it and how we feel about it. It determines how much comes into our lives.

The fear of criticism removes our imagination, self-worth and self-determination. It is the reason for many unrealised dreams and stops many of us from fulfilling our lives. It can come from people who are either "well-meaning" or just fearful of somebody getting "ahead." Symptoms include inferiority complex and lack of ambition and initiative.

Fear of poor health attracts poor health or causes it to worsen. Hill talks about the effect of the media on people during the time of the Spanish Flu. Ask yourself how much the blanket coverage of Covid 19 affected people during 2020 and later. Suggestions of reacting to various vaccines have probably caused many thousands of people to feel sick after having it. Evidence shows that negative thoughts are the initial stage of many people's sicknesses and symptoms include hypochondria and susceptibility.

The fear of getting older combines with poverty and loss of freedom to cause symptoms such as talking about yourself as "getting older" or "losing my memory." Once we start talking about ourselves, we start seeing "signs" of this, worsening the problem.

Fear of Death is the fear of what happens to you when you pass away. Religions have talked about eternal hell or fire and brimstone, which doesn't sound appealing. The reality is that we don't know what happens. However, because the laws of physics show that energy cannot be destroyed and we are energy, we know that death is only really a transition to the next stage. Symptoms here include talking about death and the lack of desire for achievement. You are the master of your domain, and you have the power to think whatever you want and, above all, be happy and grateful with your life. Fears are just an obstacle.

Chapter 16 The Devil's Workshop

Many things influence our state of mind, and negative influences are the most dangerous. Please realise that we all have fears and faults (imagine that) and are susceptible to suggestions. Set your habits up to defend against this and think and act for yourself. Don't expect anything, especially trouble, and socialise with people who are positive thinkers. Do the self-analysis questions on page 344 to find out more about yourself. The only thing that we can control is our thoughts; it is important to know yourself properly. Self-reflection helps here. By believing that anything is possible, you'll see that the only limitation is your imagination.

Read the 57 Alibis on page 351 and realise that these start with 'if'. Helpful for all of us - is not to start any sentence with 'if.' Many of these alibis give us an excuse not to do something when that something could change our life. It doesn't produce anything productive. Imagine to yourself, if you used the time more positively, what could you achieve?

"Think and Grow Rich" was a book ahead of its time. The concepts haven't changed over 90+ years and, if anything, can be used more now as current generations have more opportunities to fulfil their dreams. The research compiled by Napoleon Hill on the successful people of his generation over 20 years is unlike any other done to my knowledge.

I have read this book multiple times and found something different every time. The copy I have is the 71st edition, so there may be some discrepancies with the page numbers that I have used. A must-read for anyone who wants to "Think and Grow Rich."

CHAPTER TWO

The Richest Man in Babylon – George S Classon (1926)

This book follows some people's lives in ancient Babylon and highlights the points about wealth and wealth creation. The people involved in these stories initially struggle with life and then notice how successful people get by. The lessons, of which some are painful, come from the successful mentors who show that life isn't as hard as it appears. Some of these "lessons" take years to reach fruition, as changing one's mindset can take a long time for some. The book's key theme is that money is plentiful for those who understand the simple rules of acquisition. And there are also rules for keeping the "riches" that you achieve.

I won't discuss any of the actual characters or their actual lives in my summary here. The stories are interesting, and the characters are authentic, and anyone who reads these will be better for it. The stories are written in the language of ancient Babylon, which adds to its appeal. The rules for success in Babylon are the same as ours are in the 21st century. After selling millions of copies of this book, it is still available in paperback or Kindle.

Step 1 Start Thy Purse to Fattening

"For every ten coins, I put in, spend just nine." This is a very simple point, but for many of us, a hard concept to do. It means to save 10% of what you earn. If all of us did this, nobody would have a lack of money. Consider what you have earned in your lifetime and work out what 10% is – you'll realise that most of us would have more than enough for any retirement. In our current world of wanting it now, buying it, and paying later, this concept is more difficult for most. Do I need this now, or do I want it now? There is a massive difference between the two.

Step 2 Control Thy Expenditures

"That what each of us calls our 'necessary expenses' will always grow to equal our incomes unless we protest to the contrary."

"Confuse not the necessary expenses with thy desires."

Have you ever noticed that it doesn't matter how many pay increases you get, you still don't have money left? As a general rule, we tend to spend more as we earn more. It is almost like, "I have earned this, so I will spend this", or "I need this to make myself feel better." It won't, but many of us still do it. Having an automatic savings plan where the increase in your wage goes straight into it would be one way of preventing this.

Study thoughtfully thy accustomed habits of living. Herein may often find certain accepted expenses that may wisely be reduced or eliminated. Work out which expenses are "necessary" and others possible through the expenditure of 90% of thy income. The keyword here is necessary. Necessary can take many forms to many different people. The basics of food, shelter and clothing are necessary. Education is necessary; however, the amount spent on this varies considerably from one person to the next.

The second "cure" for a lean purse is to budget thy expenses that allow us to have coins to pay for thy necessities. The key here is to pay for what we enjoy in life and satisfy our desires without spending more than 90% of what we earn.

Step 3 Make Thy Gold Multiply

Gold or money in your purse/wallet (or a standard bank account) is gratifying but doesn't earn anything. It is a little like a safety blanket, which can make you feel good but doesn't achieve anything.

Our wealth is not defined by the wallet or the bank account but more by the income stream that the money produces. This income stream needs to be constantly flowing so that the "wallet" always has something in it. In other words, our money needs to be consistently working for us and producing more income. An example of this is the difference between having money in a bank account and having money in banking shares. For well-performing banks, the shares will produce an income stream that exceeds any interest that a bank will pay its customers for the privilege of having your money. If you are not sure about this, look at what money in fixed interest accounts will earn against shares or owning rental properties.

Step 4 Guard Thy Treasures From Loss

The first principle of any investment is the protection of the principal. Don't lay it all on the line like a bet at the casino. An example of this is government bonds, where the principal is guaranteed.

Don't get carried away by getting rich quick schemes. If something sounds too good to be true, then more than likely, it probably is. The phrase "patience is a virtue" is undoubtedly true here. Wealth can be obtained quickly, but as a general rule, it takes years. Investments in property and shares can have periods of immense growth and downturns. Still, they will be better than cash and out-strip inflation as a general rule.

Loaning money to people, especially relatives, can be dangerous. Ensure that whomever you are lending to has the ability and honesty to pay back the loan. If you are loaning money based on "just wanting to help out a friend", be prepared to be disappointed and lose what you have given. Many parents, particularly in Australia, are becoming a guarantor for their kids when buying a house. The goal of helping is noble but be aware of the potential pitfalls.

Before going into any investment, be fully aware of what it is and any of the potential dangers that go with it. Getting a "hot" stock tip from one of your mates or the cab driver and diving straight into it isn't a great idea. If you can't understand the investment and the person selling it can't describe it to you easily, stay away from it. Some property investments which provide guaranteed rental income are an example. Ask how is the rental guaranteed and for how long, and what happens after the guaranteed period finishes. Rental guarantees usually have been "built into" the price. Don't trust advice from people who aren't experts, such as don't get legal advice from your local baker. When trusting someone, make sure that they know what they are talking about and know if there is self-interest involved in any transaction.

Step 5 Make Thy Dwelling a Profitable Investment

This chapter is basically about owning your own home to reduce the cost of living. This seems like an impossible dream for many, but owning your home outright (with nothing owing on it) should be a goal of anyone retiring. Paying rent or a mortgage in retirement makes life difficult. In many countries worldwide, the one thing you don't get taxed on is your principal residence, so it makes sense to exploit this as much as possible.

The primary variable here is the amount you spend on your house. There are many extras for a house (pool, media room, tennis court, etc.) that are nice, but would some of the money be better invested somewhere else? Again, as with many things, ask yourself, "what do I need?" and work from there.

Step 6 Ensure a Future Income

This explores providing an income for your family's needs, including against unforeseen circumstances. Income streams may include rental properties, stock/mutual fund dividends, or revenue from a business venture. Another example is superannuation, which has differing effects depending on where you live. It is about having your money work for you rather than working for money.

Step 7 Increase Thy Ability to Earn

Using your strengths to keep studying and become wiser, thus becoming more skilful to reach your potential, is shared here. We all have strengths, which we need to take advantage of and make the most of what we have. Continual learning helps us in so many ways and is something that we should continue doing until we pass on to the next stage. For many reasons, we need to do this, but the major one is so that we keep our minds active in later years.

"Good luck" comes to those who take advantage of the opportunities that come by us. Those who are aware of our surroundings tend to have more good luck than others who are not. When bargains are presented to us, we must purchase them as long as we are convinced that the bargain is good for us. Good luck will be a dream for those of us who procrastinate regularly. Procrastination doesn't help us, but many of us use it because we are in fear. Fortune/good luck will always favour the brave or people who believe in action rather than just thinking about it. Too much thinking, or second-guessing ourselves, will never beat those who go for it and do it. It is particularly true for investing in the stock market or when opportunities in business arrive.

5 Laws of Gold

1. Gold/riches cometh gradually and in increasing quantity to any person who saves at least 10% of their earnings (before tax) to create an estate for their family's future. It is amazing

what 10% + compound interest results in 30-40 years later. One of the world's wonders is compound interest, but it is usually thought of as boring.

2. Gold works consistently and contentedly for the wise owner who finds a profitable use for it. It makes your money work for you rather than you doing all of the work for it. Use an investment strategy that will be consistent and work for a long time with little risk. Don't be tempted by getting rich schemes.
3. Riches tend to stay with people who invest with caution under the advice of wise men. Trust those with knowledge and little self-interest in your money. Don't believe in performance guarantees, as nobody can see the future. Past performances don't mean that the same performance will continue. Past performances are merely just past performances and nothing else.
4. Investing in a business that we don't understand or in fields we have little knowledge of leads to failure. Listen to your advisors when they give you advice, and stay away from ventures that don't make any sense to you. If somebody can't explain how the venture works or how it makes money, then stay away from it.
5. Investing in high-risk strategies and the promise of a quick fortune never works. Avoid getting involved with people who set up such strategies. These strategies will "promise the earth" and deliver very little. It's always better to have a slight amount of caution with investing rather than having a significant amount of regret. By investing and using your skills, you can maintain protected investments. Nothing ever runs smoothly, but if we limit our exposure to high-risk investments or disreputable schemers, we will always end up in a good position.

Remember that wherever thy determination is, that way can always be found – so determine what you want in life, be persistent, and your success will happen. It may take longer than you think, but with patience, it will happen. Don't be in a hurry to make your fortune.

The Gold Lender States 3 Rules

1. Keep 10% of all that you earn. By always having this money you can look after your family or loved ones in the way you want to. Less than 10% saved makes everything more challenging, and compromises must be made.
2. Don't get caught up in spending money that you don't have – you will pay for it in the future. Never spend more than 70% of what you earn, as it should be enough to live on for the necessities of life. It's interesting that insurance companies now use 70% as a standard figure for income protection. They have worked out that 70%, for most people, is enough to live on.
3. Live within your means. 20% of what you earn should be enough to pay for your debts for things like a housing loan. A car loan is a luxury that is best avoided here as it is a depreciable asset.

There are many other "gems" inside this book, and the interesting stories of the people of Babylon are very relevant for us in the 21st century. The basic principles remain the same - we have more temptations than ever before. So do yourself a favour and read the book and become the richest person in Babylon (or wherever you live).

CHAPTER THREE

The Science of Getting Rich – Wallace D. Wattles (1910)

This is one of those books that you would probably find hard to find if you looked for it in a bookshop. It appears to be a small and unremarkable book from the outside that belies what is written inside. It could be dismissed as lightweight at just over 100 pages with 17 small chapters. It is anything but this.

Many of the leaders in the self-development industry owe so much to the writings in this book. "The Secret" (Rhonda Byrne 2006) is a very successful example.

The book talks about the never-ending abundance of the universe, which is available to those who respect universal laws. Without these laws, abundance won't be easy to access. As Wattles writes, anyone can get rich, and so can you. You need to follow the principles which allow prosperity, and those principles will become automatic habits in your life.

Chapter 1 The Right to be Rich

Rich can mean wealthy, spiritual, or have supreme health. Everybody can develop oneself within them, which is only limited by our imagination. To be content with less is all on you. We have the means and resources to develop our bodies, mind and souls. How we do this and how much we do this is up to us. We need to give ourselves time to read and learn, travel the world, see how others live, have meaningful relationships, and love ourselves and others. To aspire to be rich can be everyone's goal.

Chapter 2 There is a Science of Getting Rich

Like there are sciences like chemistry and physics, there is a science of getting rich. Read that sentence again and let it sink in.

Getting rich is not a matter of where you live, what profession you have, doing things a certain way or saving every penny you earn. If it were, more of us would already be in that position. We have all seen gifted people get rich while people with no apparent gifts also get rich. What advantages we have when we are born have little to do with it. Starting off rich or poor is not as important as doing things in a certain way to ensure success. Money is just money, which can be obtained when you have very little.

Chapter 3 Is Opportunity Monopolised?

Our success is not determined by others monopolising wealth. Things can be harder or more challenging but not impossible.

Owning your own business opens up more opportunities. The internet and online businesses are the fields of the greatest wealth and success. Here there is an abundance of opportunities to build wealth. One must realise that there is abundance for all as there is no shortness of opportunities. There is no limit to what we can't see, as nature provides endless possibilities as it is constantly growing.

Chapter 4 The First Principle in the Science of Getting Rich

Our thoughts are our true power when it comes to creating. We all have the amazing ability to form things with our thoughts and thus cause the things we are thinking about to be developed. In other words, to think about the TRUTH regardless of where that leads us. We must learn the ability to think (whatever we want) irrespective of our environment.

It isn't easy. However, once we master this, all doubt and fear will disappear. In other words, we can then get what we want or become who we want to be. Learning how to develop our thoughts into what we want will cause them to be created. Doubt is the killer of all progress. It is why this book starts with the absolute acceptance of our beliefs.

Chapter 5 Increasing Life

The constant growth (abundance) of nature and the universe is where our thoughts need to be. Every thought we have causes us to expand our knowledge of our existence. So, in a way, getting rich makes it easier for us to learn and live more. This, in turn, causes us to know more and then become richer. Our environment makes it natural for us to succeed. Getting rich to buy "stuff" isn't really what this is about. Getting rich to learn and expand you is.

Many people believe that God (or the universe if you don't believe in God) wants us to struggle and sacrifice ourselves for others. What is happening is that God wants you to succeed for yourself and make the most of yourself. That may then mean you can help others.

We mustn't compete with others; rather, we are to create our wealth. We don't have to take things away from anybody as there is abundance for all. We need to create value for the people we interact with rather than just taking their money. Wanting to have what others have is not conducive to wealth. Help others to help yourself. Just read the ten commandments from the bible, and you won't go too far "wrong." To make riches at the expense of others never works in the long term. Look at your world as limitless, and riches are coming thick and fast towards you.

Chapter 6 How Riches Come to You

Giving value to others in business and life causes wealth to come towards us. Remember, a business should NOT be about winning; instead, your world will grow by giving value.

When you want something or need it to happen, form the thought that it already has happened and have the faith that it is already yours. Then it will come. It doesn't make a difference whether they are big or small outcomes. In one way or another, we have all been conditioned to believe that living in poverty and self-sacrifice is what God wants. And to ask for money or happiness is not right. It is based on scarcity, which doesn't lead to wealth or happiness.

Chapter 7 Gratitude

Being grateful for who you are, where you are, your surroundings and even the water you drink needs to be part of our daily lives. Doing this keeps us in close harmony with creative thoughts. Living life in genuine gratitude is extremely powerful as this brings us close to the source of the universe, which then attracts wealth.

Gratitude is the attitude. When we think about the negative side of life, we prevent the positive from happening. Being grateful and giving thanks consistently brings positive actions toward us. Don't waste your time or energy getting worked up by what is going on. Be aware of what is going on in the world, but don't become part of it.

Chapter 8 Thinking in a Certain Way

To achieve what we want in life, we must have a clear and definite picture in our minds of what we want. It has to be clear. Otherwise, the universe becomes uncertain of what you want and delivers nothing. Clarity is important, repetition not so much. There also needs to be a clear path towards your objective and the unnerving faith that you have already succeeded. To make this faith even stronger, feel as many of the five senses as you can; what you see, hear, smell, taste, and touch make it more real. Also, remember the gratitude for your situation.

Chapters 9 and 10 The Will Chapters

These chapters are about using your willpower to achieve success without causing any influence on others. It means - we only use our willpower on ourselves.

As mentioned previously, having a clear picture of our successful future self and having faith with positive thinking is essential. Any doubt or disbelief here will only sabotage our future goals. Fears and worry will only attract negative outcomes, and thinking of the opposite of what we want won't help us. Thinking of poverty or how sick/disadvantaged some people are bringing this negativity to you. Help the poor by becoming rich instead. The poor don't need charity; instead, they need inspiration. It's a bit like you can give people fish, and you will feed them for a day, or you can teach them to fish themselves and have food for life. Your thinking and your words are the keys to achieving all of this.

Keep your mind fixed on your goals without being distracted by the negativity in the world. There is much good in the world to focus on instead. Good health and wealth come to those who think positively about these things. By using non-competitive methods, you can inspire others to succeed as well.

As individuals, the best thing we can do is be happy and make the best of ourselves. It is hard not to smile when you are around those who constantly smile. Some social media can be beneficial, but most of it won't be. Please stay away from negative media (unfortunately, most of it is negative) and limit the amount of social media interaction as it doesn't serve you well.

Chapter 11 Acting in a Certain Way

This chapter focuses on maintaining your goals (vision), sticking to these goals and keeping your faith while expressing your gratitude. Our thoughts and actions have to be in sync with each other. Sounds easy, doesn't it.

Staying in the present and not concerning ourselves with the past or the future is critical here. We use our actions to change our surroundings in step with our goals. Imagine yourself doing what you want to do and being successful and then becoming that person.

Chapter 12 Efficient Action

Efficient action is doing what we need to do to become a success—in other words, making a habit of what we need to do each day to reach our success. Being strong and consistent with our actions will make us rich. Inconsistency will lead to the opposite. There is far more to this chapter than this.

Chapter 13 Getting into the right business

The right business for any of us is the one in which we use our strongest abilities and something natural for us. Enjoyment of this work is essential, as we will always do better at something we want to do.

Accept change and take your opportunities when they arise, as they always will. When doubt arises, as it inevitably will, take your time and have gratitude that the solution will come. Being in a hurry to achieve brings fear and negativity and is best avoided.

Chapters 14 and 15 Increase and Advancing

An increase is a fundamental part of living in the universe. Mankind has to keep increasing with everything until life has ended. We desire a more abundant life, so the abundance and increased message must be conveyed to everyone you meet in business. It will, in turn, give an increase to everyone around you. However, it is important to be respectful of others when you are doing this.

In any field that we choose to be in, it is necessary to show our faith and purpose to others that we will succeed. It then rubs off on others in the same way. When doing your job or working in your business, work with the point of view of advancing yourself and having clear goals. Others then will be attracted to you, and opportunities will arise. Take these opportunities to advance when you can, when your gut tells you to. Be guided by your gut.

Chapters 16 and 17 Observations and Summary

Our governments tend to keep most of us living in Struggle Street, as we don't know how to succeed. However, if people are constantly advancing, then they will obtain success. People who get rich on the competitive plane by squashing others don't help anyone, and their success will be limited. The more of us who get rich on the creative plane, the better.

Think of riches as unlimited, and don't concern yourself with potential potholes in the future. Only focus on what is in front of you today. With positive thinking (today), solutions arise, and tomorrow's problems don't seem as difficult.

Be careful with your thoughts and your speech. Try not to speak of disappointment or insurmountable challenges, which will attract failure. Be confident in your abilities to do what you need to do.

Get into a habit of being grateful. We must keep a clear mental image of our goals and dreams and have gratitude for what we have. An easy way of doing this is to appreciate the water you drink every time you do so. The water signifies life while hydrating you.

Keeping ourselves active and constantly advancing will bring us to our goals. The Science of Getting Rich gives us how to achieve our success and riches. Please read the book a few times for it all to sink in and buy the original, as it contains much more than I have written here. It is undoubtedly an easy book to read with easy to follow steps.

Other authors have used these steps during the last 100 years. With this in mind, keep smiling, remain positive, stay in the present and be grateful for all the wonderful things in the world.

CHAPTER FOUR

The Millionaire Next Door (1996)
Thomas Stanley and William Danko

This is a book that was about twenty years in the making. The research was conducted on more than a thousand people, many of whom were millionaires and high-income earners. And in 1996, it was much more challenging to reach the million-dollar figure than in 2022 (an accurate comparison today would be 3 million). This research examines many wealthy people who don't appear rich on the outside. Where and who the wealthy people of America are will be a surprise to many. But not as much to the wealthy themselves. This book highlights the seven main traits common to those of the wealthy. The figures that I will be quoting from the book are from the 1990s, so they are a little dated about today's wealth. However, the concepts are still as strong as when they were first written. My copy is from 1998; there is a newer update from 2010. It is, not surprisingly, a US and worldwide bestseller.

One of the first lines in this book is that "wealth is not the same as income." Nearly half of the wealth of the US is owned by 3.5% of our households. That is not a typo – 3.5%. It is a compelling and simple statement that is what the heart of this book is.

More than 32 million households in the US have incomes greater than $50k, and almost a quarter of them earn more than $100K, yet most of these people live paycheck to paycheck. What follows is that just over half of the wealth is owned by 96.5% of our households. Since 1996, does anyone think this has improved?

Financial assets tend to appreciate, and while buying your home isn't a foolproof financial move, it sure is better than purchasing multiple cars and renting property. 65% of households have equity in their own home (desirable). Yet, more than 85% of households own more than one vehicle (not desirable) as cars depreciate as soon as you drive them out of the car yard and keep on doing this for their life span.

Of the millionaires in this study, 80% have accumulated their wealth in just one generation, and they did it slowly. It is the most effective way of achieving this accomplishment. The chances of obtaining instant wealth through sport, entertainment or choosing the correct lottery numbers are less than 1 in 4000. Just contrast this against the top 3.5% of households with more than $1 million in equity. These people are generally businessmen who have lived in the same town all their adult lives. They typically own a small factory, a chain of stores, or a service company. And the key throughout is that they are married and remain married. Although this book generally talks of the wealthy as being male, there is no reason why the wealthy cannot be female (substitute male for female and vice versa). Couples need to stay together for financial security – divorce is an absolute killer of financial success.

7 Traits of millionaires:

1. They live below their means – spend less than they earn. It sounds basic, but many of us don't do it, live on credit (or buy now pay later schemes), and buy something that we can't afford to make us feel better. And in the 2020s, there are many more "things" that we can buy than in the 1990s. Cars and clothing would be the most damaging in that period. I would add phones, the internet, and online gambling to it to update this list.
2. They allocate their time, energy and money efficiently in a way conducive to building wealth. They make their money work

for them. They invest in themselves to improve their knowledge to improve their chances of success. And they keep on learning to an advanced age.

3. They believe financial independence is more important than displaying high social status. More than likely, they would buy a Toyota rather than a Ferrari. Also, they don't live in the more affluent parts of a city where house prices are through the roof and "keeping up with the Jones's" is far more costly than living in average suburbia.
4. Their parents did not provide economic outpatient care. Their parents would have been "fair" and instilled sound values rather than giving their kids a deposit for a house (or buying a house for them) or paying for expensive university studies.
5. Their adult children are economically self-sufficient and can look after themselves after leaving home without relying on their parent's money to survive.
6. They are proficient in targeting market opportunities and making the most of what is needed globally. There are opportunities everywhere; we have to be aware of these and make the most of them.
7. Some occupations have more upside than others. They choose the right occupation. Some fields require long hours and hard work, whereas others require fewer hours and less hard work. Also, ask yourself, "will this occupation still be needed in 20 years?" You can always change your occupation, but it is easier to choose the right one earlier.

Building wealth requires discipline, sacrifices and some hard work. It doesn't just happen by itself. Most millionaires DON'T own expensive clothes, watches or cars etc. And remember that only a minority of millionaires ever lease a car. About 2 in 3 millionaires are self-employed people, while only about 20% of people are self-employed. They are also far more likely to have lived in the same house for twenty plus years, while only 17% of the people attended a private school. Interestingly, 55% of their kids go to a private school as the wealthy see value in good education.

Most millionaires make their own investment decisions, and about 20% of their wealth is held in stocks or managed funds. They have more in their pension fund or superannuation (401K). How to determine whether wealthy - "multiply your age times your realised pre-tax annual household income from all sources except inheritances. Divide by ten. This, less any inherited wealth, is what your net worth should be."

Generally speaking, PAWS are builders of wealth while UAWS are spenders. To be a PAW (prodigious accumulator of wealth), you should be worth at least twice the expected level of wealth. To be a UAW (under accumulator of wealth), you should be worth half or less the expected level.

Interestingly, about 90% of millionaires never received a gift from a family business. A study done in 1892 showed that at least 80% of the "rich" didn't inherit much.

Ancestry seems to make a significant difference. The greatest number of millionaires are Russian (22%), Scottish (20%) and Hungarian (15.1%), while those of an English background is way behind at 7.71%. However, time spent living in the US tends to level the performance. It may be being accustomed to the US style of living, causing these groups to spend more. Russians, largely, are managers/owners of businesses. The Scottish are frugal, and while their incomes are not typically high, they make up for this through discipline and financial independence.

Frugality is the most important trait of the wealthy. For couples to be successful, both the partners have to show the same constraints. When trying to establish a successful business, this is especially true. To become affluent and STAY affluent, we need to:

1. Operate on an annual budget and stick to it.
2. Know how much you spend on the necessities of life (not necessarily Netflix).
3. Have clearly defined sets of yearly goals for your lifetime.
4. Spend a lot of time planning your financial future.

It means we need structure and goals without which we are aimless. The really wealthy minimise their taxable income by whatever means legally possible while maximising their unrealised income (wealth/capital appreciation). An example of this is Ross Perot, who had a net worth of $24 Billion, and his annual income for 1995 was about $230 million. However, he only paid about 8.5% tax on his income, whereas most people would pay around 30%. Most genuinely wealthy measure their success by their net worth, not their realised income. The point here is that having a high net worth is not taxed in most countries, whereas income is always taxed and taxed heavily for high earners.

Accumulating wealth is far easier if you don't live in a high-status neighborhood. Houses are far more expensive, local government taxes or higher rates, and even insurance costs are different. The main reason for living in a place like this would be to keep up appearances, which is a very common human trait. It is necessary not to have a mortgage that is more than double your household realised income to become wealthy. Do not borrow more than $200K if your family's income is less than $100K. Starting in a high-status neighborhood is very difficult to achieve.

People who are prodigious accumulators (PAW) tend to spend nearly twice as much time planning and strategising their investments than under accumulators of wealth (UAW). The high-income PAWS are less likely to hold degrees in Law or Medical Fields than UAWS. Also, they are less likely to have student debt issues. People in Law or Medical fields tend to spend more on material "things" keeping up with their fellow graduates or people in their neighborhood. UAWS will spend money on services that control their families' spending habits.

There is an inverse relationship between the time spent purchasing luxury items such as cars and planning one's financial future. There is a saying, "you are where your focus is", and if your focus is on cars or suchlike, then there is less time and energy spent on your finances.

Cash doesn't earn anything (low interest) by itself. UAWS are twice as likely to hold more than 20% of their net worth in cash, whereas PAWS have wealth in businesses, real estate or equities. Gold or Crypto is similar to cash in this regard but with much more volatility.

How much money we have or how much we make is just like a report card. Who we are shouldn't change with how much money we have or don't have - our values in life should stay the same. Money only gives you more options on what you can do with your life. As a general rule, Millionaires tend to buy a car of average cost and buy it outright.

There are many different ways to spend your money without even thinking about it. It is far easier to earn a lot in Western countries than accumulate wealth. However, the key is no matter where you live, whatever your income is, always live below your means.

The most frequent gift that millionaires receive from their parents is tuition. Some received support in buying their first home, while others received an interest free loan. The interesting thing here is that the more money help adult children receive, the less likely they are to accumulate their wealth. It is almost like a subconscious thing to NOT produce their wealth and instead rely on their parents. Conversely, the adult children who are given less will accumulate more. On page 203, there are ten rules for affluent parents and productive children, and this is required reading for those who want the best outcome here.

Who are the affluent? Most of the affluent are business owners, including self-employed professionals. What kind of business do they own? It would seem that all different types of businesses are owned by the wealthy. The most crucial factor is the character of the owner. Change does occur in types of businesses that do well, which is the one constant in all of this.

The success of "The Millionaire Next Door" comes from the authors conveying the stories of the millionaires interviewed and making sense of the copious data they have obtained. I have left the stories (which are the best part of any book) and copious data out of this summary. Read them for yourself when you buy this book. To my knowledge (and I have known to be wrong!), this book is one of a kind in the way it has been put together. The information here is solely based on US figures but is relevant for many who live elsewhere. People are very similar in many different countries. Putting this information together in an interesting and thought-provoking way is not easy. I would call this book the number one defensive strategy book of wealth management ever written (that I know of). Defence is an important strategy left out of most wealth management books but is critical if you will be "The Millionaire Next Door."

CHAPTER FIVE

The Art of War (Sun Tzu) ~513BC

So what does a book about war have anything to do with you? Two and a half thousand years ago, Sun Tzu was a great military strategist. His writings about war caught the attention of the king of Wu (ancient China), Ho Lu. His teachings led the armies of Wu to many great victories. They have been used extensively in China over the centuries, with even chairman Mao using them for similar purposes.

"The Art of War" was translated to English by E.F.Calthrop and Lionel Giles in the early 20th century, resulting in 2 versions. From this, many other versions were written. Most versions will have 13 chapters which describe the teachings of Sun Tzu. The book has been used by Napoleon, Patton, Macarthur, Stalin, Schwarzkopf and Castro in war, to name a few.

The teachings have also been used by Dr Henry Kissinger, Jack Welch (GE), Larry Ellison (Oracle), soccer's Felipe Scolari (Brazil), the NFL's Bill Belichick (Patriots) to John Buchanan (Australian Cricket). There has even been a movie of the same name. In the film "Wall Street", Gordon Gecko quotes Sun Tzu regularly when teaching his apprentice Bud Fox.

I will attempt to convey the message of "The Art of War", which, although relatively short, is difficult to summarise. It is far easier to buy it and read it yourself to grasp the message. My copy has 13 chapters. Think not of war when you are reading this – instead, think of the competitive edge I can receive and what that is.

Chapter 1 Laying Plans

Five constant factors are taken into account.

1. Moral Law – follow your leader regardless of any danger.
2. Heaven – environmental conditions such as night/day, hot/cold, and seasons.
3. Earth – the terrain in front of us.
4. The Commander – virtues of wisdom, courage, sincerity etc.
5. Method and Discipline – preparation and the maintenance of the army (team) and the budget needed.

These points need to be known by our leaders if victory (or goals) is to be achieved. Then make comparisons between yourself and your enemy (like a SWOT analysis).

Use the art of deception, be prepared and do the unexpected. Above all, keep your tactics to yourself.

Chapter 2 Waging War

There are 20 points to this chapter, all dealing with managing your "war". In sports, this can be used in competition finals and business, achieving an edge over your competition. These points are more like a do/don't list.

Some points to consider:

1. As we have all heard about stupid haste in war, being clever is not about having long delays. While long delays can mean resting, procrastination of ideas rarely wins. In other words, any action is better than nothing. Fear of ideas doesn't help any business. Try/test and try again is better and will get you there eventually.
2. Have you ever heard of a sports team complaining of a very long season and being jaded at the end? No country/business/sports team has ever benefited from prolonged warfare. Keep

yourself and your staff fresh. Give them regular breaks from work and make the job more enjoyable.

3. Bring your supplies with you, but use the enemy's supplies. Then your "army" will have enough. Always use your enemy's assets when you can.
4. To win, our "soldiers" must be well motivated, and there must be rewards for their success. In other words, more motivation for all.
5. In "war", let victory be the primary goal, not having a long campaign. In other words, long elections are rarely good.

Chapter 3 Attack by Stratagem

In "war", it is better to take the enemy whole and intact. To shatter your enemy serves no good purpose as there is nothing left to take, and never destroy your enemy. It could be argued that a good example of what not to do would be what happened at the end of WW1 whereby it led to a second war.

Excellence in war comes from breaking your enemy's resistance without actual fighting. It's never a great idea to lay siege on walled (or protective) cities.

Long takeovers are expensive, morale deflating and take your mind off the main game of running a business. An example of this would be a long, hostile takeover. The skillful leader wins without fighting, without laying siege and without lengthy campaigns.

A rule of "war"; is if our forces are 10 to the enemy's 1 to surround them. If 5 to 1 to attack them. If 2 to 1, divide our "army" into 2; and if unequal, flee. Being ignorant of your team causes instability and indecisiveness for your players. If your troops (players, staff) can't obey you, retreat. In other words, be aware of your strengths and weakness and play within these.

If you know your enemy and yourself (without ego), you will win most of your battles. If you know yourself but not your enemies, you will win half your battles.

If you know neither, then you will lose most of your battles. Knowing yourself first has always been an excellent place to start.

Chapter 4 Tactical Dispositions

The clever fighter excels at winning with ease while making no obvious mistakes. By doing this, defeat becomes impossible (or near enough to), and the opportunity of victory will be high. Planning is important here.

Chapter 5 Energy

How you control a large "army" has the same principle as that of control of a small "army". Both direct and indirect methods are used to ensure victory. Using both in combination can lead to an endless number of moves. Having more moves (options) is critical. An example of an indirect method would be showing no emotion - conveying an indifference to the opposition about what you want to achieve.

Energy may be likened to the bending of a crossbow, while a decision is compared to the release of the trigger. Sometimes we only have to bend. The simulated disorder shows perfect discipline. Simulated fear shows courage, simulated weakness reveals strength and hiding orders underneath a cloak conceals strength. The clever leader looks to the combined energy of many, not so much the individuals.

In other words, the combined strength of a team is usually more than just the parts.

The energy from good "fighting" people comes from the momentum of a round stone rolled down a mountain from thousands of feet. That is to say, having great people around you rubs off on the rest of your organisation.

Chapter 6 Weak Points and Strong

Impose your will on your "enemy", but don't allow your "enemy" to do this to you. Meaning - control your outcome and don't let others control what you are doing.

Go to places where your enemy has to hasten to be ready and where you are not expected. Whoever is first on the "field" and waits will be much fresher than the second person who has to hasten to get ready, leading to exhaustion. It is better to be prepared for what happens next than racing around like a "chook with its head cut off". Namely, make life difficult for your opposition and don't do things the same way. Where we intend to fight shouldn't be evident to our enemy. Be vague about your intended direction, making it hard for them to plan against you. This way, they will have to be prepared in many places, thus spreading themselves out thinly.

Compare your opposition with your team so that you will know its strengths and weaknesses and use what you have to your advantage. Do not repeat your successful tactics repeatedly; always modify your methods to keep your opposition guessing.

There are 34 points in this chapter. This is only a sample.

Chapter 7 Manoeuvring

Having put together your team, it is vital to mix and harmonize the different elements before proceeding. In other words, we need to put together a team that works together rather than just having good individual people.

Don't wait until everything is perfect; use smaller parts of your force (team) to set the agenda. Waiting for perfection is asking for trouble; test your oppositions' readiness to play YOUR game. Don't enter into alliances until fully aware of their intentions. It is important to know what everyone (involved) wants. Some people may appear as "friends" but become something else.

Use caution if you are not too sure. We must be familiar with and aware of what dangers lie in front and the terrain ahead of us - otherwise, we shouldn't lead. Using local guides with their local knowledge who know the specifics of what lies in front of us is essential to take advantage of the country.

Ponder and deliberate before you make a move. Stop for a "second" and think about what happens when you make a decision.

A clever leader avoids their opposition when their spirit is high but attacks when their spirits are low. Studying the mood of your opposition is critical to success.

Likewise, it is unwise to uphill attack your enemy and not engage them when they come downhill. When things are not in your favour, wait until they are. When you surround your opposition, leave them a way out and do not press a desperate foe too hard. If your opponent becomes desperate, they will "fight" harder, and you will lose far more than you need to. Remember, a win is a win, regardless of how much you win.

Chapter 8 Variation in Tactics

Play your own game and focus on your team and how well prepared they are. Don't rely on your opposition showing up, but rather be ready if they arrive. Also, make yourself unassailable; rather than chance them not turning up.

Always be ready to seize an advantage and consider both advantages and disadvantages. Play to your strengths and conceal what weaknesses there are.

There is never just ONE way in which to be successful. There will always be oppositions that we don't attack, avenues that we shouldn't take and positions that are best left alone. The leader must understand the different variations available that would best serve their team.

Chapter 9 Army on the March

During warfare, camp in high places - putting yourself in the best position available.

Position yourself so that any danger is in front of you (preferably low) and that safety is behind you. Ensure that you know where the threat is and meet it on your terms.

Always leave a safe "getaway" at your disposal.

Take the high and sunny positions during battle so that the light shines into your enemy's eyes. Take the best position, leaving your opposition in the worst position. Please stay away from cliffs, confined spaces, crevasses, and quagmires during the battle and let our enemies take these positions. In other words, reduce your potential risk and let your opposition take all risks. When an enemy is quiet, they rely on their natural position, so be wary of this if they are unusually quiet/ inactive. It is during these times that they are at their strongest.

Peace proposals without a signed agreement indicate a plot planned. Unless someone has signed an agreement or officially conceded, there is still more to come.

The sight of your team whispering in small groups, or speaking softly, point to disunity in the ranks. Conversations in secret with your team members that others aren't part of lead to less teamwork and more chance of failure.

When in training, people follow commands and be well disciplined. If not, then discipline will be poor. Teams play the way that they have been trained. Refer to the early story in the book about concubines and Sun-Tzu's reaction to this.

Chapter 10 Terrain

This chapter deals with the natural advantages of terrain in warfare and the dangers within your force (team). At first glance, these points only seem to be of benefit in warfare. However, many team sports that have physical contact can benefit. Have you ever noticed how some well-disciplined teams play well above their current form and defeat teams with better credentials? These teams follow their leader (or coach) with their predetermined game plan and don't deviate from it regardless of the individual's thoughts. Another example of this is to use the sun (behind you when at its lowest) and the wind (when you know it gets stronger as the day goes on).

Chapter 11 The Nine Situations

Sun-Tzu recognizes the nine types of ground and how a team should play these to its advantage.

In your territory, fight not. In a hostile environment, don't stop any advancement, and on the contentious ground, do not attack. In sport, don't go for the big play coming out of your half.

When it is advantageous to, move forward. If not, stay where you are. An example would be in a bidding war - bid higher when you need to but never bid against yourself.

Take advantage of "stealing" something of importance from a strong, orderly enemy. It will make them more inclined to deal with you and your will. "Pinching" opposition staff members would be an example. Always take advantage of your unprepared opposition and attack the unguarded. For example - where a team is going to blitz on a first down in the NFL, thinking the opposition is going to run, but the QB changes the play at the last second and throws deep.

Study the well-being of your team and conserve your energy and strength. People in desperate states lose their sense of fear and perform at their best. Having reached his destination, Cortez burned his ships so that there was no return from where they were which is an excellent example. Getting the best out of your strongest and weakest team will determine how the leader responds to the situation.

Constantly changing your plans prevents your enemy from anticipating your moves.

Don't enter into alliances until we know their plans – it's always best to understand what your "friends" are thinking.

Tell your team your objective, but never tell them your design. Also, tell them nothing if the situation is dire.

If an enemy leaves a door open, you must rush in and take advantage of their mistakes.

Chapter 12 Attack by Fire

When Sun-Tzu wrote this chapter, a fire was meant to be fire, gunfire or explosions. Fire, for our purposes, can be an aggressive takeover, an aggressive marketing campaign, an attack on the unexpected or an all-out attack when a more cautious approach is usual. The easiest example of this is the NFL's fake field goal/fake punt. Teams routinely use the punt on the 4th down when they are going nowhere. But very occasionally, they surprise their opposition by using a fake version, which carries more risk but has more reward.

Stay behind the “fire”, but don’t get caught up in it. Use the “fire” with an intelligent move, but be ready to use “water” to aid your movements. In other words, be prepared and use what resources you have.

Always proceed with caution, ensuring that your team/organization will survive whatever you do.

Chapter 13 The Use of Spies

Good information is key to everything. Having good knowledge of your organization and your strengths is essential. Spies can be your opposition staff who feel not valued by their current employer. Spies and capturing them can be used to understand your opposition and use it to your advantage. Also useful is having decoy spies that spread disinformation and ousting them to your opponent.

Using subtlety with your spies throws your opposition off. Spies aim to control information and the use of deception.

I have left many other concepts to read when you buy this book. Sun Tzu’s ideas have many applications. These are particularly evident in business, sport, warfare and politics. If your field is one of these, the concepts here are very powerful. As the knowledge of Sun-Tzu’s philosophy has become recognized further, there have been many instances in the last 100 years where his concepts have been adopted. Think not of this book as being about warfare but more about how it can aid your journey through life.

CHAPTER SIX

The Wisdom of Florence Scovel Shinn (1925 – 1940) 4 Complete Books

For all of the 15 books that I have summarised in this book - this collection of books from Florence Scovel Shinn was most effective for me on money and wealth. I first read this book two years ago on the recommendation from Jim Fortin. I have a copy sitting on my desk at work (I am an optometrist). This and being part of his TCP (Transformation Coaching Program) has changed my life. Both of which I am extremely grateful for. It also 'made' me re-read all of the other books and apply the principles to my life. If you are not where you want to be in life, then, more than likely, money has a large part to play in all of this. You may not know this yet, but after reading Ms Shinn's book, you will understand what I am talking about. For the non-religious reading, which may be annoyed by the references to Christ and the Bible, insert 'the universe' as this is probably another accurate way of looking at this.

Book 1 is titled "The Game of Life and how to play it." Florence Scovel Shinn (FSS) was widely known for her excellent healing work and assisting people with their problems. These books use the old and new testaments to demonstrate the rules of life with utmost clarity. Jesus Christ taught that life is a great game of giving and receiving; "Whatever a man soweth that shall he also reap."

This translates to - whatever we send out via words or action will return to us; what we give, we will receive. So if we give hate, we will receive hate; if we give love, we will receive love.

We are also taught that imagination plays a crucial role in the game of life. We must train ourselves to imagine only good things – health, wealth, love, and friends.

Our subconscious mind has to be directed by us (i.e., deep feelings or clear images) to carry these actions out. Our conscious mind "sees" life as it appears to be – death, disaster, sickness, poverty, and possible limitations. It then goes on to influence the subconscious.

"There is a place you are to fill, and no one else can fill, something you are to do, which no one else can do." In other words, what we put into our minds will determine which path we will take. We have the power ourselves. Many of us are unaware of our true destinies. We strive for situations that aren't there, which leads to failure.

Jesus said, "By your words ye are justified, and by your words, ye are condemned." It is a significant quote as many people have brought disaster into their lives through their words. Our subconscious has no sense of humour (and no comprehension of sarcasm), and people often joke themselves into unhappiness.

"Ask, and it shall be given, seek, and ye shall find, knock, and it shall be opened to you" (Matthew 7.7). Meaning - every desire, uttered or unexpressed, is a demand.

Fear of lack, failure, sickness, loss, and insecurity is man's greatest enemy. We must imprint the subconscious mind with positive/good realisations. "Why worry? It will probably never happen." Worrying is a worthless emotion. It only can achieve negative results.

"All things whatsoever ye ask in prayer, believing, ye shall receive." You must act as if you have already received it. Imagine yourself being the person already that you want to be.

IMPORTANT: If one asks for success and prepares for failure, they will get the situation they have prepared for. FSS interlaces these comments with stories that confirm these ideas. When you read this book, you will see what I mean.

The horseshoe, rabbit's foot, or any other 'lucky' item contains no power. Still, man's spoken word and belief that it will bring him good luck creates expectancy in the subconscious mind and attracts a 'lucky' situation. So, the power lies in believing that it will bring success, not the item itself.

There is an old saying that man only dares to use his words for three purposes, "heal, bless or prosper." What we say of others will be said of us, and what we wish for another, we want for us. In other words, "Curses, like chickens, come home to roost". Our only enemies are within ourselves. We must have peace and harmony. We are open to prosperity when we are truly at peace and harmony. Being critical of others blocks us from prosperity. Goodwill produces an aura of protection about us when we send it.

"If you don't run your subconscious mind yourself, someone else will run it for you." This means better being in control of your subconscious rather than letting external circumstances control your life. Be the person who sends out only goodwill to everyone and who has no fear and cannot be influenced/affected by the negativity of others around themselves.

FSS talks of the laws of non-resistance when she says, "I have a wonderful work, in a wonderful way, I give wonderful service, for wonderful pay." You could do a lot worse things than repeat that to yourself every morning before going to work.

The law of Karma states that we only receive what we give (Boomerang).

On page 31 (Kindle version), we are shown that Christ's teachings indicate that the subconscious is where we can fight adversity. The mind is more powerful than we give it credit for. This means that doubt and fear can bring about adversity and a 'light' mind (no doubt and very little fear) brings about prosperity. Doubts and fears can poison the mind and our body, attracting disaster and disease. There are many stories in the book that confirm this. One of the stories is about a man who has "cancer" but "heals" himself by changing his thoughts.

To impress the subconscious, active faith is always essential. It is said that there is no peace or happiness for all of us until we have erased all fear from the subconscious, and that fear is misdirected energy.
Jesus said, "Why are ye so fearful, O ye of little faith?" We have to tell our subconscious that success and money are plentiful and have no thoughts of losing. One can only contract germs while vibrating at the same level, and fears drag us down to the germ level. Our fears are just a waste of emotion for all of us.

Real love requires selflessness and no fear. Jealousy is the enemy of love. When people are happy, they can become selfish, and the law of Karma then starts to act.

We suffer through a lack of appreciation and gratefulness. People can't attract money if they feel it is evil. Many of us stay in poverty by saying things like "money means nothing to me", "I don't need any money", or "money is the root of all evil." By believing in abundance and having no fear, we will attract money. So, not believing and having fear attracts negative actions in your life and a lack of money. Obviously, love and goodwill are invaluable in business, and conversely, sorrow, regret, and remorse are the opposite. People who come across as happy and positive usually do well in business, as this is the type of customer they will attract.

Society has conditioned many mothers to worry about their children.

They are told that they are not good mothers if they don't. Today, these worried parents, known as 'helicopter parents', are then responsible for their children's many diseases/accidents. Ask yourself, "how have I helped my children by worrying?" The answer will usually be "not much." Instead, stay in the divine mind (positive and peaceful) and worry less about your kids.

Have you ever heard "Ask, and you shall receive?" When giving gifts/money, it must be with love for "God covet a cheerful giver." When one has made their demands from the universe, we must be ready for surprises. Things don't always come to us in the way we think. I find that having no expectations of people/circumstances helps here.

Creating Divine Design (P49) is a process of demanding definite leads, and the way will be made easy and successful. However, we shouldn't force a mental image as with many things. Forcing most things never helps—a bit like when you have trouble remembering something. We are better off forgetting about it, and it will come later, rather than forcing something that will frustrate us.

Or when we try to force a square peg into a round hole. We need to demand divine design to come into our conscious minds, leading to inspiration. Then we begin to see ourselves making great steps forward. This is all easier when we are at peace with ourselves. An important note is that parents should never force careers and professions on their children. As parents, we think it is "our" responsibility to ensure that our kids take the right path. Kids need to lead their own path, and happiness will come. Again, fear stands in the way.

Anger (fear) blurs our vision, poisons us, and is the cause of many diseases and us making 'wrong' decisions that lead to failure.

Fear and worry lead us to the things that we fear. We also must be cheerful receivers and givers. If we aren't, we are blocking our (energy) channels, which can lead to having very little, or nothing at all. Like most things, we must have a balance of giving/receiving to have a positive life. "The Lord loveth a cheerful receiver, as we do a cheerful giver."

If we desire something (P55), we need to make the demand for it. Most of us tend to limit ourselves in our demands, and as a result, most of us get less. (There is a perfect story on this page that you will enjoy when you read the book). Continually affirming the demand establishes the belief in the subconscious. Again the fear of loss can lead to a picture of loss in the subconscious. Our subconscious is essential, as this is the real driver of our brains.

"One should always follow a denial with an affirmation." Jesus said, "Whatsoever ye ask the father, in my name, he will give to you." Fearless faith, non-resistance (go with the flow), and love are the rules of life. On page 61, there are examples of denial and affirmations, which are powerful.

"Your Word is Your Wand" (Book 2)

Your spoken words and your thoughts are most influential in determining your path. Be at peace, be happy and be positive with your words. Success comes from gratitude and having fearless faith. Have an appreciation for the many things around you which serve you differently. A series of affirmations concerning this on page 67 is good to read and powerful to use in your life.

Prosperity comes from the belief that all things are possible. An affirmation of this would be, "Infinite spirit, open the way for my great abundance. I am an irresistible magnet for all that belongs to me by divine right." Imagine that you are a magnet for money, and success will come.

Happiness comes from having no fear, apprehension or dread (helped by having no expectations). Love comes from the love of everything and happiness. Marriages work best when two hearts beat as one. Affirmations that help with love and marriage are on page 79. Read them as these affirmations are easy to learn and use.

Faith is far more powerful than hope. To a large degree, Faith will influence how we act in life. Hope just wishes for something without anything behind it. Many people will confuse the two and feel that hoping for something will make it magically happen. It more than likely won't happen. As with debt, we should deny it, and things will come to you. That may not be what our initial thoughts are, but to allow a loss to overcome you doesn't really achieve anything. And as there is no loss of memory in the divine mind, we will only forget what is not good for us. I was listening to a podcast recently, and Rhonda Byrne (Author of "The Secret") said on her path to wealth when she received a bill, she turned it around to feel like it was money coming in. So a bill for $100 is thought of as $100 coming in. This is a way of denying debt, and feel as though there is actually money coming in.

When we are harmonious and happy, we are healthy and have the opportunity to be wealthy. Sickness comes from sin. Being unhappy for long periods doesn't serve us at all. Many of us cause ourselves to be sick by our thoughts. Jesus said, "Be thou healed. Your sins are forgiven."

With poor vision (I'm not talking about your eyesight), we have fear and suspicion and live in the past or the future. Many of us are thinking about what is next and not enjoying the moment. We need to live in the now, enjoy it, and be grateful for what we have.

With poor hearing (listening skills), we practice stubbornness and tend not to hear things that we should. We are actually 'hearing' what we want to hear. There are large discrepancies between groups of people listening to precisely the same thing, as it brings a lot of conflicts. There is a vast difference between listening and hearing.

Heart disease comes from fear and anger. Fear and anger serve no purpose for us, only heartbreak. With a divine mind and being at peace, there is no scarcity or fear.

When we dislike/hate things, we create a vivid picture in our subconscious and then it materialises. Our words and feelings are powerful when it comes to manifesting our future. It is much better not to have such strong feelings about those things.

Thinking in extremes results in adverse outcomes. So to manifest the good, consider these thoughts with an open and generous mind. One of the secrets to success is enjoying your work and having a great interest in it. The Chinese say, "A man without a smiling face must not open a shop." And "even honesty won't help you without a smile." We attract the things that we give a great deal of thought to.

I have deliberately left out the affirmations of Ms Shinn's work (buy the book and read them). However, one stands out "The unexpected happens. My seemingly good now comes to pass." This is particularly powerful as it stops the argument from our analytical mind.

All life is made up of vibrations, and when we vibrate to success or happiness, we attract things that we want. Feel rich and successful, and you will be that way.

Envy and resentment will achieve the opposite, so negative thoughts must be left behind.

By paraphrasing the scriptures of Mark and Matthew, we get "when ye pray believe ye have it. When ye pray, ACT as if you have already received." Read that a few times to really understand it and its simplicity.

The spiritual attitude towards money and wealth is to trust in God and never voice a lack or limitation. The divine idea for all of us is in abundance, and this is the way to think of everything good. In other words, believe in the infinite universe where there are endless opportunities and wealth. Keep on noticing beautiful things, and they will come into your life. This is why it is important to be grateful for the things in your life every day. It is a potent habit to get into. Initially, try something simple like being thankful for a glass of water.

Nothing is too good to be true; nothing is too wonderful to happen and nothing too good to last when you look to God for good. We all have to realise that we have the power to choose our thoughts. When it comes to a time for you to decide, ask for a definite unmistakable lead, and you will receive it. What we have to realise is that all big ideas have some opposition. Just don't let others change your mind. Remember, they can only change your mind if you allow them. We can control what we think, but we must do this without forcing it. This is so much easier without emotion and when we have a relaxed mind. Abundance comes to those who think of no limitation and no lack. Always feel abundance (with peace); it is very powerful.

"The Lord is thy Shepherd. I shall not want" (Psalm 23). This statement implies that infinite intelligence can supply us with every need. We need to believe that this is the case. Once we truly understand this, we don't need to hoard possessions as they are all on our pathway.

Through the following few pages, references to Psalms and Isaiah bring powerful messages that we all need to read. And you will find an analogy to "Snow White and the 7 Dwarfs" interesting. On page 274, we are asked to think about what form your cruel stepmother is talking about in your subconscious and how this affects our freedom. We must never let our stepmother cause all of these negative thoughts.

The final book is the power of the spoken word. Without going into detail, which would spoil the explanation of this last chapter, the topics talked about are

- Weapons ye know not of
- I give unto you power (Luke)
- Be strong; fear not
- The glory of the Lord (Psalm)
- Peace and prosperity
- Your big opportunity
- In nothing be anxious
- Fearlessness
- Victory and fulfilment

Read all of these at your own pace.

Florence Scovel Shinn's final book was published after her passing. Her affirmations are the most critical parts of her writing and what you will get the most out of when you read the book.

This is the sort of book that could be missed easily in a bookstore, but that would be a mistake. Ms Shinn is very spiritual and may have too many references to the bible for some readers. Still, her work is extremely rewarding to those who take on board her lessons. If we can live our lives in the way that Florence Scovel Shinn suggests, we would all be wealthier and happier in many ways, and the world would be full of peace and joy.

CHAPTER SEVEN

Who Moved My Cheese? *(Dr Spencer Johnson) 1998*

The Author, Dr Johnson, has written many books of the same type. The most famous of those is the "One Minute" series. It sure packs a punch for a book that is under a hundred pages and only slightly larger than a large mobile phone. The ground-breaking series is co-written with Kenneth Blanchard, Larry Wilson and Constance Johnson.

The power and influence are best illustrated through the testimonials at the start of the book. What is this book about? And why does it have an unusual name? Essentially this book is about change. Change is something that is moving far more quickly than ever before in our history in the twenty-first century. Whether we like all of the changes is not the point. Those who can adapt to the world changes will flourish, whereas others who can't cope won't do as well, which is why this book has been so popular and is used by so many people to deal with the change in their lives. Whatever size company they may be a part of or just an individual making their way in the world - change affects all of us regardless of whatever we do.

So what explains the cheese part? Cheese is a metaphor for anything that we want to have. Cheese could represent a job, money, relationships, material possessions, freedom, health, spirituality or even world peace. As humans, we all have different beliefs and opinions about what is important in our lives and the world. And anyone reading this will have a different idea of their cheese or what it looks like.

As we all know, change can be stressful, but it doesn't have to be that way, and this is what the book addresses. What can be more stressful is the action of sticking your head in the sand and hoping that everything will work out by ignoring your surroundings. Change can also involve opportunities that can arise when the inevitable change happens.

Successful people love change, as it often creates an opportunity. At the same time, it equates to fear for the most general population. Consider the Covid world of the last two years where our governments and media have widely promoted fear. It hasn't all been doom and gloom as many people have made some serious money while others have hidden under the bed.

This book doesn't take long to read, yet it has the potential to impact whoever reads it hugely. You will discover this when you read it for yourself.

There are three parts to this book:
The first part is 'the gathering', where several old schoolmates talk about the change in their lives. Having just been to my own fortieth year school reunion, I can relate to this part. It was amazing to consider the different paths we all went down, our decisions, and where we had all ended up. The interesting thing is that we currently have very little to do with what we achieved at high school. Don't let school define where you are going, as it is just a small chapter in your life.
The second part is the actual story (the largest section by far), which, when you read it, will leave a smile on your face, which is never a bad thing. I won't reveal this part as it is the most interesting, and I don't want to spoil it for you.

The third part consists of the discussion the old schoolmates have about the story. It is interesting to observe these friends' different interpretations of the story, which demonstrates how people's own beliefs and opinions are influenced differently. The important thing here is to be aware of our own biases and respect others and their opinions even when they 'fly in the face' of our own. It's a bit like life in general, where people's beliefs are formulated by their upbringing and surroundings and then influenced (with their own bias) by our changing world.

The story of "Who Moved My Cheese" is about four little characters who run through a maze looking for the "cheese" to make their lives easier and happier. Two of them are mice called "Sniff" and "Scurry", and the other two are little people (of the same size as the mice) called "Hem" and "Haw." Each day, they search for the cheese they want using different methods (as we all have our ways of doing things). Using their strengths (we all like to do what we are good at), they found what they were looking for each day. As the story moves forward, the situation in the maze changes (where their cheese becomes harder to find and harder to get), and this is where the behaviour of the four characters changes in different ways.

"The more important your cheese is to you, the more you want to hold on to it." That is to say - we don't want to let go of anything important to us, which can mean many things. Relationships, beliefs, material possessions and things that "keep us safe" are all things that can have importance to us all. But do these things help us in the "game of life?"

The mice do less thinking and more doing and adapt quickly to the situation. In comparison, the people complain about the unfairness of the change and do nothing initially. Hem and Haw are very human in this regard. Many of us wear the "complain" badge like a badge of honour.

"If you do not change, you can become extinct." Even though Hem is afraid, he changes his thinking and starts acting differently. Haw doesn't change what he is doing as he feels too fearful. Fear is probably the main reason many of us aren't proactive. Our brains keep us "safe" by not changing anything and doing what we are in the habit of doing. Many people don't like being fearful, but that is what many people are.

"What would you do if you weren't afraid?" The answer to this is probably anything that you want to do. It's a bit like me in writing this book. I had the idea for years but procrastinated about doing it. That was just my fear, and the reality is that it was all in my head. Once I started actually writing, the fear disappeared, and I enjoyed it. "When you move beyond your fear, you feel free." So true, and enjoying life follows from this. We all have fears, which are all made up in our heads when we think about it. Fear prevents us from genuinely living; living with fear is merely existing.

Think of someone in your life who lives like this. We all know people who live that way, yet their lives don't have to be like that.

"Old beliefs do not lead you to new cheese." Realise that beliefs/ opinions are your inner programming, and most beliefs are not based on fact despite thinking so. Changing your beliefs and being open to new thoughts opens up your world and opportunities. Ask yourself, "how do I benefit from my current beliefs?" The answer is - you probably don't.

To find out what happens to the characters in the book, you will have to read it yourself. After reading, ask yourself, "do I live my life like this?" The answer is probably, as we all do it from time to time. Being aware of it is a start to changing how we live.

The book's best quote is, "Move with the cheese and enjoy it." Whatever you have in life, be grateful for it. Enjoyment from life comes from moving along the path of your choice, not someone else's.

The discussion at the end (which is important) puts all of the book's ideas into real-life situations. Different people identify with each of the four characters, which reflects life. Remember, there are no wrong or right opinions of any person - they are what they are. After reading it, the best thing that anyone can do with this book is to share it with others. Even for a person that doesn't like reading, this book is an easy read. Books don't have to be lengthy to be effective, which is one of the best examples of this. To find your 'cheese' in life, maybe you need to follow some of the principles these little characters embody and change yourself.

CHAPTER EIGHT

The Intelligent Investor (1950) – Benjamin Graham

This book has multiple revisions, which were first published in 1950. My copy is the 2003 edition. I prefer this version as it has written commentary at the end of each chapter by Jason Zweig. He makes Graham's concepts easy to understand. Also, this version has a preface and an appendix written by Warren Buffett.

Who was Benjamin Graham? He has been called 'the father of value investing' with his principles. He has been the inspiration for many successful investors. His most famous student is Warren Buffett. As Warren has never written a book on investing, this is the closest you will ever get to understanding his principles.

Why is this important? Well, suppose you seriously want to get ahead in the world financially (and make life easier for yourself). In that case, I can see four ways of doing this. The options are to have shares, property, own a successful business, or have exceptional talent. A talent such as Michael Jordan, Serena Williams or Tiger Woods (most of us mere 'mortals' don't have that). If the share market is your path, this book is 'the guide' – otherwise, as Buffett regularly says ', just buy an index fund.'

There are 20 chapters in this book, which I will attempt to pull in to align with the theme of this book. But without reading the whole book, you are doing it an injustice.

Graham's core principles include:

1. The future value of every investment is a function of its

current price. The higher the price you pay, the lower your return will be. Anyone who listens to Warren Buffett would hear him talk about "there are no bargains out there at the moment", as this is one of his key values – buy low and keep.

2. By insisting on the 'margin of safety' – never overpaying, no matter how exciting an investment seems, many other buyers will jump into investments while Buffett bides his time.
3. In the end, how your investments behave is much less important than how you act. Graham says throughout his book that he is not a fan of the airline industry (Buffett as well) for investing purposes. But he points out that you should never succumb to the certainty that one industry will outperform all others in the future. Qualities of an intelligent investor are being patient, disciplined, and eager to learn; you must also be able to control your emotions and think for yourself. Don't just follow the herd. The herd can come in many forms – one is the share market itself. Just because a stock has become popular and its price has risen dramatically doesn't mean that it is worth its price. An example of this would be Enron, which collapsed dramatically in the early 2000s.

"An investment operation is one which, upon thorough analysis, promises safety of principal and an adequate return." There are three elements of this:

1. You must thoroughly analyse a company and the soundness of its underlying businesses before you buy its stock.
2. You must deliberately protect yourself against serious losses.
3. You must aspire to 'adequate', not extraordinary, performance. An investor calculates what a stock is worth based on its business value. A speculator gambles that a stock will go up in price because somebody else will pay even more for it. In other words, don't be greedy and be as realistic as possible. On

> a personal level, I bought Blackmores shares (ASX) in the early 2000s after doing my due diligence. In contrast, the dividends paid were good (>5%); the share price didn't move for years and stayed in the range of $15 to $25. It is a good company, but the returns weren't great. In early 2015, everything changed. Blackmores is a vitamin and supplement company that suddenly became very popular with Chinese people in Australia and China. The share price escalated, and within three months had gone from around $20 to $100, at which point holding my shares didn't make any sense (from a logical point of view), and I sold. Within the next few months, the share price rose to $170 before the "inevitable" crash. Depending on how you look at it, I either sold at a good time or sold way too early. The point is not to be too greedy and leave something there for the next person. Could I have done better? Sure, but if you are happy with your trades, that is the best you can ask for.

In 1973, a typical shareholder held a stock for five years before selling it. By 2002, this time had dropped to 10.9 months. By now (the 2020's), this time would have dropped even further. Are we that impatient? Or are we better traders? The answer, like always, is probably in the middle. Suffice to say that Graham would not have been a fan of day trading.

Graham says never risk more than 10% of your overall wealth in speculation. Never mix this money with your more risk-averse investments. In other words, speculation is okay, but don't put your house on it.

Inflation must be taken into account when measuring your investment success. Most of the time (78% up to 2002), stocks outpace inflation. Since this book was written, the last few years have seen periods of historic low inflation and the share market progressing well. For US investors, allocating 10% of your retirement to TIPS (treasury securities) is an intelligent way to keep your money safe and ahead of inflation. However, there are no guarantees that stocks will outperform bonds or cash. Be wary of any guarantees with a stock tip. The value of any investment is, and always must be, a function of the price you pay for it. Meaning what we pay for an investment is critical. The only thing you can be confident of in forecasting future stock returns is that you will probably turn out to be wrong. Graham is convinced that a 50-50 (stocks/bonds) split is the best for a defensive investor. It allows the investor to feel like they are making moves in the market while still having a safety cushion. The most sensible bond purchases for many years were the US savings issues. High yielding bonds are best avoided for the ordinary investor.

Graham says there are two ways to be an intelligent investor:

1. By continually researching, selecting and monitoring a dynamic mix of stocks, bonds or mutual funds (active) or
2. Creating a permanent portfolio that runs on autopilot and requires no further effort (passive). It is the best option for the person who doesn't want to put much effort into research.

Everyone should keep a minimum of 25% in bonds, as this gives us a cushion to keep our poorly performing stocks when (not if) they drop.

100% stock portfolio can work only if:

1. You have enough cash to support your family for one year.
2. You will be investing for at least 20 years.
3. Survived bear markets of 2000, 2008 and 2020 and did not sell stocks in these markets. Bear markets always return – it's a bit like yin and yang. It is always harder to not sell when the prices are plummeting. During the early days of the pandemic, my portfolio (100% stock) dropped by 30-40% within 2-3

months. I didn't sell anything, and the stocks recovered over the next ten months. You have to believe in the process.

Bond funds can offer cheap and easy diversification and the convenience of monthly income. Other investments include securities (did you see the movie "The Big Short"?). These are best purchased from companies like Vanguard, but if someone tries to sell a derivative of a mortgage security like a CMO, run for your life.

Annuities, again, are best purchased from someone with low costs, like Vanguard. Their name will appear regularly here as their costs are generally low.

Preferred stock is another investment to avoid.

4 Rules for selection of Stocks (Shares):

1. An adequate diversification (minimum ten stocks, maximum 30 stocks).
2. Each company selected should be large, prominent and have low debt levels.
3. They should have a long record of dividend payments.
4. The investor should limit the price they will pay for a stock (PE ratio) over the last seven years. Growth stocks are the ones that will double their share earnings in 10 years (i.e., over 7.2% annual growth). 'Rule of 72' is handy to estimate the time money takes to double - divide the growth rate into 72. For example, an investment with a growth rate of 6% will double in 12 years.

Graham's guide to owning 10-30 stocks and not being overexposed to one industry is a way of mitigating your losses. It can also reduce your profits, but you can't have it both ways. Index funds are another way of avoiding restless sleep for long periods. Index funds work very well with regular monthly investing of $100 or more; during even the worst bear markets. They take the guessing part of investing OUT. Second-grade bonds and preferred stocks usually perform poorly in bear markets. An example is World Com 2001. Today these are called junk bonds and are best avoided.

A requirement of the intelligent investor is the ability to avoid stockbrokers selling new stock during bull markets. It is all speculation. It is easy money. For every dollar you make in this way, you will be lucky if you only lose two.

Day trading – holding stocks for less than one day – is one of the best weapons for committing suicide or at least losing most of your hair (male or female). With day trading, the more you trade, the less you keep. Sometimes, trading will make money, most will lose, but your broker will always win. For some, with so little knowledge behind them, you may as well play roulette at a casino and gamble on red or black.

An important lesson is "don't just do something for the sake of doing something." The best move is when you don't do anything in most cases. No matter how many other people want to buy a stock, you should only buy it if it is a cheap buy into a desirable business.

With IPOs – it's probably overpriced; imaginary profits only; insider private opportunity; idiotic, preposterous and outrageous. These are more of a leap of faith sometimes. Ask yourself, what am I buying? There are no numbers to base your decision on.

An important thing to realise is that a great company is not a great investment if you pay too much. Look for great stocks that are temporarily unpopular. These can always be found; it may take more time to do so. Be patient.

Having some foreign stocks (including those in emerging markets) can help insure against the risk of your backyard going backwards. It has become far easier now with access to global markets and ease of trading platforms.

Every investor who owns shares/stocks must expect them to fluctuate in value over the years (just like housing). Don't get involved in the share market if you don't like some uncertainty or fluctuations. Day-to-day or month-to-month fluctuations aren't a genuine concern to a dedicated investor. Look at things over medium to long term periods. Don't believe the forecasts of what the market will do in the next 1-2 years (crystal ball gazing).

To determine the book value of a company's shares, go to the balance sheet and subtract 'soft' assets such as goodwill, trademarks and other non-physical items. Then divide by the number of shares. The anomaly of all of this is that the more successful the company, the greater its share price fluctuation. The better a company's record and prospects will contradict the book value of a share. This is probably why Buffett never bought technology stocks for many years, as they would rarely meet this criterion.

The stock market often "gets the price wrong", so investors need to keep an eye on the basics of the companies that they hold. Base your stocks on real data and sell them when it makes sense.

Speculators can profit from market fluctuations (up or down). Investors buy and hold their stocks at the right price; "Never buy a stock immediately after a substantial rise or sell one immediately after a substantial drop." There sometimes is no rhyme or reason why stocks do this. Remember, people with emotions control the stock market, so just because a stock price is rising doesn't mean anything.

Mutual Funds

1. The average fund's performance doesn't cover the costs of running them.
2. The higher the mutual fund expenses are, then the lower its returns.
3. There can be an expectation to constantly do something (trading) when sometimes it is better to do nothing. The more frequently a fund trades, the less it tends to earn. Remember that mutual funds have staff that have to justify their position.

Performance index funds (particularly those with low costs) outperformed 80% of the market. Index funds are, by definition (trying to mirror the general performance of the market), boring; however, boring is usually very effective.

When to sell mutual funds:

1. When the strategy of the fund unexpectedly changes dramatically.
2. There is an increase in the expenses of the fund.
3. Large tax bills have become common.
4. Sudden erratic returns (this can be from positive or negative returns).

Whose advice do you take? Pay attention to the advice and recommendations from investment banking houses, particularly those with a good reputation.

Use your own judgment if you know what you are doing. If, however, you don't know what you are doing, you need advice - and advice that doesn't come from your local cabbie. Unfortunately, advisors with credentials mean very little. The phrases "guarantee", "sure thing", and "can't lose" are examples of warning words that you should stay well clear of.

How do we determine the future?

We can't, however, consider the following:

1. The company's long-term future.
2. The quality of its management (this can change rapidly, so beware of change).
3. Financial strength and capital structure (large debt levels have to be financed somehow).
4. Dividend record (companies that give dividends will usually give dividends, whereas companies that don't usually won't).
5. Current dividend (compare this against previous years, and if this is showing a pattern of dropping, this isn't a good sign).

These points are crucial to the investor and are well explained in chapter 11. It is a critical chapter, as you will agree with me as you read it yourself.

Chapter 12 deals with reading earnings reports - sounds fascinating, doesn't it? When reading financial statements, watch out for words like 'special charges' or 'non-recurring expenses or earnings.' Phrases like these can distort a company's earnings and make it appear more profitable than it actually is. And if you aren't paying attention, these misses can cost you in the future. Unfortunately, some companies are very good at hiding stuff in a report. So don't place too much emphasis on just one year of earnings.

To avoid bad stocks:

1. Read financial reports backwards. The bad stuff is usually hidden at the back. Some reports are deliberately long as to put off anyone reading them. It's a bit like the terms and conditions of having a credit card. Who actually reads that?
2. Read footnotes in the annual report.
3. Read about financial reporting and find out as much as possible about a potential company.

Chapter 13 compares four companies, which to the casual observer, appear one way. Still, the opposite becomes true for the value investor after close analysis. Graham applies his principles that highlight that 'value' companies to invest in aren't always the most attractive to look at. Important reading.

Chapters 14 and 15 highlights the steps needed for the defensive and enterprising investors. For the defensive investors, steps are laid out on page 348. For the 'lazy' defensive investor, buying into a stock market index fund is best. You get diversification, which is relatively safe and a reasonable return.

For the enterprising investor, the basics are the same, just modified, as shown on page 385. Key strategies for the enterprising investor:

1. Buying companies at below net-current asset value.
2. Realise that history has demonstrated that yesterday's losers are often tomorrow's winners.

If you don't enjoy the sound of dissecting a company (and would rather have root canal work done), buy an index fund. It sounds like a broken record, doesn't it?

For those hungry for greater success, being disciplined and consistent is essential, and believing in what the figures say rather than going by what the share market is doing at the time.

Chapter 17 deals with the case history of four very interesting companies with 'highs' but eventually finished in tears. Graham shows that the signs of this were, in fact, evident well before the slide. These "types" of histories can be seen in the technology crash of 2001 and later in the GFC downturn in 2008.

Chapter 18 compares different pairs of companies by using figures without emotion. This is interesting as it shows the stock market fluctuations in the face of reality. In this chapter, Graham indicates that over-valued companies can stay for years, making guessing the stock's direction challenging. The commentary chapter shows similar stories from around 2000 to 2002.

Chapter 19 talks about dividends, or lack of them, from certain groups of companies that thought that most profits should be ploughed back into the business. It also has a go at the behaviours of corporate managers. The vigilance of large corporations is essential not to become a victim of scandals (such as Enron in 2001). As shown on page 500, an investigation of statements from Enron could have brought up a red flag about the company.

Towards the end of this book is a transcript by Warren Buffett in 1984 called "The super investors of Graham-and-Doddsville", which offers a fascinating study of Benjamin Graham and David L Dodd. Buffett shows how their study helped him towards success. It is significant as Buffett shows the methodology that he uses. It is required reading for anyone who proposes to use value investing.

Books like this (not many like this) are required reading for share investors. Sure, there are other methods for investing in the stock market; however, if you are serious (and not into gambling) about investing, read this book.

CHAPTER NINE

Secrets of the Millionaire Mind (T Harv Eker) 2005

T Harv Eker explains in this book why some people achieve wealth easily while others, who probably work just as hard, struggle big-time. The secrets, as told here, are within us, and they are a matter of changing one's beliefs, which for many of us, have been ingrained since our childhood. This book is one to implement and includes action steps I have left out of my summary.

The author found that rich people think differently from poor and middle-class people early on. It is essential to recognise that our ways of thinking have produced us where we are now, and taking time to look in the mirror, would be of purpose here. To change, we have to be willing to let go of some of our old ways of thinking and adopt new ones.

Have you ever noticed how many people who suddenly come into big money end up losing it in a short period? Three in five lotto winners are no better off financially five years after their win. It happens because, on the inside, they are not ready for it. Externally they become rich, while internally, they subconsciously set about levelling this as they almost feel uncomfortable becoming rich. It's like growing a fruit tree – what is unseen (the roots) creates the visible (fruits). If you want to change the fruit, the roots have to be changed. We learn that there are four different worlds from which we live – physical, mental, emotional, and spiritual. Most of us only think in terms of the physical. The other three worlds are the roots. The inner three worlds also need to change for our changed outer physical world.

To change, we must declare what change we want, and we need to be specific about that. There is no point in stating that you want to be rich; instead, put an actual figure on this, such as $10 million. It is important as this creates an energy vibration throughout your body. This sends both a message to the universe and our subconscious.

We can see that "my inner world creates my outer world." A critical formula is on page 18, called the process of manifestation, which is T->F->A = R. Thoughts lead to feelings, feelings to actions and actions to results. What and where our thoughts are, and come from, is critical in all of this. Page 20 discusses how these thoughts are "conditioned" in three primary ways:

1. Verbal programming (what have you heard when you were young)
2. Modeling (what did you see when you were young)
3. Specific incidents (what did you experience when you were young)

Verbal programming includes hearing phrases like "money is the root of all evil", "money doesn't grow on trees", and "we can't afford it." These phrases can become rooted in our subconscious, where bad is associated with the rich. Once this happens and the formula is applied, the result will be that the subconscious mind doesn't "want" (to be) rich.

To change, there are four steps:

1. Awareness
2. Understanding
3. Disassociation
4. Reconditioning (In other words, change your thoughts and words to be positive about money)

Modeling comes from our environment, especially from our parents. We learn by watching our parents – did you ever hear "save for a rainy day?"

Instead of this, talk about good days and no rain; by speaking in terms of positivity and abundance that is what you will attract.

If you talk about "saving and holding on to what you have", you are promoting scarcity/fear, which will be the result you receive in your life. Some of us say things like "I will never do what mum and dad did" with anger and rebellion. This won't work as money/success becomes linked with anger, which means that whatever success you have won't bring you happiness. Once we recognise that we are plenty and successful without the fear of motivation of fear or anger, then plenty will become our new norm. Any fear rarely works positively.

Specific incidents that happen to us can lay the blueprint for our whole life. This is particularly important for couples, as money is the number one cause of breakups.

Couples need to be on the same page regarding money, and you both need to agree to live by your shared values with this. This is why talking about these issues is important early on in any relationship.

What are we programmed for? If we limit how much money you want to earn, this will become your ceiling. This means - be careful what you wish for. Page 45 "your income can grow only to the extent that you do." Also, on page 45, "wealth principle – consciousness is observing your thoughts and actions so that you can live from true choice in the present moment rather than being run by programming from the past." In other words, the past is just the past; it doesn't mean anything more than that. Live your life in the present and make your own choices.

We must choose our thoughts and beliefs wisely. Remember that nothing has any meaning except for the meaning you give it. We learn that we need to think and act like rich people to produce the results that rich people create. At the end of every chapter is the affirmation, "I have a millionaire mind."

Part 2(the most significant section) discusses how rich people think and act differently from poor/middle-class people. Rich can be subjective; what one person sees as rich won't be like another. Part of being rich, to me anyway, is to be happy - otherwise, what are you doing it for? My personal definition would be – being able to choose to work/not work while having/experience anything that you want, when you want to.

1.
Rich people believe "I create my life", whereas poor people believe "life happens to me."

Rich people believe that they are in control and poor people believe that they have none. Take the lottery (or Lotto in Australia) for an example. People in poor suburbs spend multiple of what people in affluent suburbs do playing it. The poor will be able to tell you what the winning numbers are, while the rich will have no idea. Poor people play the blame game; it's the government's fault, the economy is wrong because I grew up this way (their parents), God is not nice, etc. They never look in the mirror.

The poor will always justify their position in life and often justify their beliefs by saying phrases like "money's not important." If you think or say things like that, then money won't be important in your life, and you probably will never have enough. Try paying your bills with something other than money if you believe this to be true.

Rich people believe money is important. We need to focus on expansion, not on limiting beliefs. According to the law of attraction, when we complain, we attract crap into our lives (if you like crap, go ahead). Ever notice how people who are constant complainers/" whingers" have nothing go right for them? We are best to stay away from people like that, or you will drag yourself down with them. This can be a hard thing to do with close friends and family. Surround yourself with positive people. When you hear yourself complaining, justifying or blaming, STOP yourself as soon as possible. An important concept is "there is no such thing as a rich victim!" When we act like a victim, we get attention, which is what people want, but being happy and successful is virtually impossible while you are doing so. For me, this is the most important of the seventeen ways.

2.
"Rich people play the money game to win while poor people play the money game not to lose."

Poor people are concerned with survival and security instead of wealth and abundance. Middle-class people just want to be comfortable - whatever that means.

I certainly have been guilty of this, giving the excuse that we have enough or that it will affect our kids. I now want to be rich to do what I want to without thinking about money (this doesn't mean that my life would be much different, but it gives you options). Being comfortable doesn't give you that option.

3.
"Rich people are committed to being rich. Poor people want to be rich."

Poor people have 'files' in their subconscious that tell them something wrong with being rich. Things like:

- What if I lose money? What will my friends say?
- I will pay more tax if I earn more
- I could get robbed
- Blah, Blah, Blah!

These thoughts stop us from creating/attracting wealth. Our minds are so powerful, and negative/mixed messages are one of the primary reasons most of us never become rich. The universe can't deliver wealth to you if it is confused by your thoughts and words. And if you don't know exactly what you want, how do you expect the universe to help? When you commit to being rich, failure is not an option. Getting rich requires focus, courage, effort, a good attitude and the self-belief that you can create wealth and deserve it. Once you show commitment, the universe will help and support you in your efforts. Until you do this, wealth creation will be difficult. Writing down your wealth goals is very important here.

4.
"Rich people think big, poor people think small."

Value is the key to what you will be paid, which is determined by supply, demand, quality and quantity. In other words, how many people can you serve well?

Most people play small as fear of failure or a feeling of unworthiness takes over. Most things in life are sales. Have you ever been shopping when the salesperson comes across as desperate for your sale? Does this make you want to buy or just get out of the shop fast? People are attracted to the opposite of this. Happiness comes from being able to use your natural talents to the utmost. You need to think big, help thousands of people, and say, "I have a millionaire mind."

5.
"Rich people focus on opportunities. Poor people focus on obstacles."

How we think determines our outcomes – poor people focus on the negatives and live their lives in fear; middle-class people think, "I hope this works", while the rich say ", it will work as I will make it work."

Think about those who have significantly increased their wealth during the pandemic of the early 2020s, and think about those who haven't. Not everyone who has been in a vulnerable industry has gone backwards. Rich people will take the risk, while poor people expect to fail. Procrastination is a trait of the poor. And even though I am not poor, procrastination and inaction have prevented me from being as successful as possible. Action is essential, as the wealthy focus on what they want, whereas the poor focus on what they don't want. With the way that the universe works, the difference is vast. So, if you want to be rich (and who doesn't), focus on making, keeping and investing your money. If you want to be poor (really??), focus on spending your money.

The best way to learn about a business or an industry is to work in the one you want to be involved in. Certain things just can't be taught, as we sometimes have to fail and learn from our mistakes. Put yourself in the industry you desire to succeed in, and doors will open for you. You don't get anywhere by doing nothing. Mistakes are a sign that you are doing something. Remember, there are ALWAYS opportunities; take them when you can.

6.

"Rich people admire other rich people. Poor people resent rich and successful people."

Poor people look at the rich with resentment, jealousy and envy. It is as if they made them poor. This line of thinking doesn't help anyone. Poor people have the idea that the rich are dishonest when the reality is that a high percentage of the rich are honest (that is one of the reasons why they are rich). Being dishonest can earn you a fortune, but riches like this are rarely held for an extended period and usually end in tears. So many people have been conditioned to believe that you can't be rich and a good person or rich and spiritual. An ancient Huna (Hawaiian) philosophy is to "Bless that which you want." In other words, bless the nice things that you want instead of being jealous of them.

7.
"Rich people associate with positive, successful people. Poor people associate with negative or unsuccessful people."

This can be a source of motivation to model their strategies on others or to just be around fellow people with positive energy. Positive energy is contagious. Believing in "everything happens for a reason, and that reason is there to assist me" (even when something happens that initially seems "bad") helps you grow faster and stronger.

A word of caution here is not to judge or criticise others who don't get this, as that would make you no better than they are. Our words and thoughts are extremely powerful. There is no point in surrounding yourself with negative energy. Behaviours such as arguing, gossiping and backstabbing are best to avoid. This will bring you down, and any success will be difficult. Generally, poor people feel uncomfortable being around highly successful people. This is due to the fear of rejection. Fear prevents many of us from being successful. Be genuinely happy for anyone who is enjoying great success. When you hear of success that somebody has, think, "if they can, I can too."

8.
"Rich people are willing to promote themselves and their value. Poor people think negatively about selling and promotion."

Resenting promotion is a great obstacle to success, as marketing yourself is critical. If you think about it, everything that we do is sales, whether a relationship or your profession. Rich/successful people are mainly excellent promoters, skilled in excitingly packaging their value. Robert Kiyosaki ("Rich Dad, Poor Dad") points out that every business is dependent on selling. He notes himself as a best-selling author, not a best writing one.

One creates a lot more wealth than the other. Rich people are usually leaders who earn significantly more than followers. Beliefs are of huge importance here as you have to believe in your value and your product/service. Also, it is important to continually over-deliver to your clients to create extra value that they were not expecting with your service. They, in turn, will be grateful to you for doing this. It is challenging to sell (whatever you are going to) without these firm beliefs.

9.
"Rich people are bigger than their problems. Poor people are smaller than their problems."

Most people don't want the hassles, headaches or responsibilities of the road to wealth. Poor people see a challenge and run for the hills. Another way of looking at this is that rich people look for opportunities in potential problems. The key is not to allow problems or obstacles to remove your happiness or success. Ask yourself, "how can I turn this around?" or "what can I make of this situation?" Remember, your wealth grows as you do. Never dwell on problems; imagine yourself being able to hold more wealth and then attract more wealth. Poor people are problem-orientated, whereas the rich concentrate on the solution.

10.
"Rich people are excellent receivers. Poor people are poor receivers."

The feeling of not being good enough to receive is just a story you have made up. We need to think we are worthy and not hold negative thoughts. Some people say, "it's better to give than receive." Really? Now that is an interesting thought that serves no purpose. Who decided that one? You are training the universe not to give to you by not accepting. The rich believe that they will be well rewarded for their efforts and value. Poor people can also work hard but believe that it is wrong to be well rewarded. The important point is that "money will only make you more of what you already are."

Being accepting is not just about money - it can also be about more peace, love, and happiness. If you are a kind person, your money will help others less fortunate. If you are a jerk, or an ass, then… Importantly, be grateful for who you are and what you have become—being grateful needs to be part of our daily rituals of living. Be thankful for many things in your life, and as a result, you will be happier and at peace with yourself.

11.

"Rich people choose to get paid based on results. Poor people choose to get paid based on time."

This infers that while there is nothing wrong with being paid an hourly rate for your job, the reality is that you will never be paid what you are worth. This "security" of knowing what you will be paid comes at a price – never really making it.

Rich people believe in themselves and the value that they give. To become wealthy, you need to be paid on results. Remember, never put limits on what you can earn. Also, learn to leverage yourself or duplicate systems to build wealth. This is why many professionals (like myself being a single practice optometrist) make a comfortable income without "hitting it out of the ballpark." Many of us see expansion as painful (and it could be), but this is where you will make serious wealth. If you work for someone else, make sure you are paid a percentage of what you bring in. Otherwise, start your own business. Most millionaires own their businesses. If fear stops you from taking the opportunity to change your circumstance, nothing will change in the amount of wealth you create.

12.
"Rich people think both. Poor people think either/or."

Poor people don't believe in abundance and think you can't have everything. Rich people use a little creativity to have the best of both worlds. Think, "how can I have both?" Always think this way. Besides, where is the enjoyment of life if you can't have both? Everybody knows that you'll do better in a job you love, so why do anything else?

Money is important as it brings freedom and choices, bringing happiness. Happiness doesn't come from worrying about not having enough money. Having your cake (I prefer chocolate) and eating it sounds good to me.

13.
"Rich people focus on their net worth. Poor people focus on their working income."

Net worth is the accurate measure of wealth. Wealth comes from income, savings, investments and a simple lifestyle. Rich people spend the time and energy to learn about investing. This is where money can be made easily. Poor people only think in terms of income.

Not having an effective investment strategy makes life much harder for yourself when it doesn't have to be that way. Having a simple lifestyle also makes it far easier to be happy financially. Ask yourself, "do I really need that?" Focusing on net worth is far more important than just your income. Your focus will expand your wealth. A good financial planner can be worth its weight in gold by showing you the best financial solution.

14.
"Rich people manage their money well. Poor people mismanage their money well."

Wealthy people have supportive money habits, making it far easier to manage their money. Poor people prefer not to do this, as they prefer the freedom to do what they like. This result is that they get less freedom because of money shortage issues. The reality is that you won't get any more until you can handle the money you have.
Our habits are so important.

An easy way to gain wealth is to create passive income streams. Putting away small amounts (for example, 10% of your take-home pay) into, say, an index fund and eventually living off only the income is good. Do this without touching the capital you put in, and you can never go broke.

We have to show the universe that we can handle our finances for everything to fall into place. Balance is important, so just saving won't get your freedom. This is because (and this is like a diet) if you are like most people, you will eventually say, "stuff this", and spend all of your savings. So spending is critical to restoring the balance here. The only rule is that there is a limit to your spending, and it should be kept to. Having separate accounts for saving and spending makes this easier. Remember, money will control you, or you will control money. It's YOUR CHOICE.

15.
"Rich people have their money work hard for them. Poor people work hard for their money."

Working hard is good, but it won't make you rich. Most people in the world aren't wealthy, but they certainly work hard. Many wealthy people don't seem to work hard, and the simple reason is that they use leverage. In other words, the more money can work for you, then the less work you will need to do. You can do this by having a business (other people doing work for you) or having investment capital working for you. Rich people reach financial freedom when they can live the lifestyle they want without working or relying on anyone else. This happens when their passive income exceeds what they spend.

Without the right amount of passive income, we will never be free. Unfortunately, we don't get taught this at school (at least, not the one I went to). Knowing this, would you have made the career choice that you did? Find a career/business where creating income streams is relatively easy. Don't just get a job or go to university like everyone else. Think long term, and then you will be able to make your own choices.

Buying "things" through emotion and how you feel at the time using "other people's money (OPM)", such as banks and credit card companies, is a recipe for failure. Only use OPM to buy assets that either produce an income or go up in value or even do both (houses, shares, land, business). Buying a car (particularly a new one) with OPM is not good. Take the long-term view (and this is really the only view), as assets like houses and land almost always increase in value. Patience is an important quality here. Most rich people pick an asset class that they are comfortable with, learn it and stick to it for life.

16.
"Rich people act despite fear. Poor people let fear stop them."

Fear shows up in our lives regularly. Fear comes from having to do something that you don't want to. Are rich people fearful sometimes? Yup! However, they don't let fear stop them. Uncomfortable? Sure

- but fear can lead to success and happiness. Running away from it doesn't get you anywhere. We have to develop the habit of not being stopped by anything. If you are willing to do only easy things, life will be hard. Doing hard things makes life easy.

Being in the comfort zone is not a recipe for wealth. The more we are in comfort, the fewer chances of success. The more uncomfortable we are leads to greater success. You say, "comfort is okay", or "I like being comfortable." That may be the case, but you will never be wealthy or truly happy this way. Happiness comes from growth and living life to the fullest. Growth only comes from being outside of our comfort.

Our mind is both our most important asset and our most destructive. The stories are amazing that we tell ourselves about this and that, with little chance of fruition coming from them. We can choose what we think. I will repeat that. We can choose what we think. So why think negatively - as the result will also be negative. Remember, nothing has any meaning except the meaning we choose to give it.

17.
"Rich people constantly learn and grow. Poor people think they already know."

Don't expect a different answer if you keep doing the same thing. Growth comes from learning - nobody knows it all. Learning through reading books or doing courses is what the rich do.

The poor will say something like "I don't need it" or "I don't have the money." If you are poor, "when will you need it?" Or "when will you have the money?" If you don't change, the answer will be the same a year from now, and you will be in the same position in life.

Becoming rich is as much mental as it is physical. The best investment that we can make is an investment in ourselves. The order of success is 'Be, Do, Have.' The poor believe it to be 'Have, Do, Be.' In other words, the rich believe that BECOMING a successful person first is the most important. Whereas the poor believe that if I HAVE a lot of money, then success will occur. There is a titanic difference between the two thoughts.

This book has many concepts in it which are easy to follow. There are exercises to complete at the end of every chapter (not listed here, buy the book), which are critical to your improvement. Knowledge is important, but applied knowledge is gold. Commit to the seventeen wealth files, and life will improve. Re-read this book multiple times and do the exercises. You will find yourself answering with different responses each time. The responses will change as you will change. We all need to be a little better for the world to be a better place. Buy the book and start your journey.

CHAPTER TEN

The Tao of Pooh (Benjamin Hoff, 1982)

An unusual title, describing Taoism through the eyes of A.A. Milne's favourite bear – Winnie the Pooh. Who really can say that they dislike Pooh bear? This topic dives into living without preconceived ideas about how life "should" be lived. The oldest book on Taoism was written by Lao-Tse, who believed that the more man interfered with the natural balance of the universe, the further away from harmony man became. The more forcing he did, the more trouble he found himself in. From the Taoist point of view, sourness and bitterness come from the interfering and unappreciative mind. Life itself is sweet when it is understood and utilised for what it is.

The essence of P'u (the uncarved block) is where things in their original simple form contain their natural power. This can easily be spoiled or mislaid when simplicity is lost. P'u sounds like Pooh.

This book is written as the author talking to Pooh and his friends and understanding "The Tao of Pooh" in how Pooh understands life. Even though Rabbit is clever, whereas Pooh is not, Pooh says, "that's why he never understands anything."

For many of us, we are too clever for our own good. This is probably because of the modern concept of "being right all of the time." Eeyore doesn't understand as well, as his complaining attitude gets in the way of wisdom and happiness. Do you know anyone like this? When you get rid of arrogance and the complex nature of life (and what it can bring), you will discover the simple and fun secrets known to those as the "uncarved block." Pooh is the "uncarved block."

We can enjoy the simple, quiet, and natural when we are in the "uncarved block" state. At this point, we can do things without thinking and make them work. As Piglet says, "Pooh hasn't much brain, but he never comes to any harm. He does silly things, and they turn out right." The character of Owl in "Winnie the Pooh" is seen as a scholar. This is useful from a Confucius's point of view, whereas the Taoists write, "the wise are not learned; the learned are not wise." Being someone wise can bring many things to you, but peace and happiness probably won't be part of it.

Pooh doesn't think about the day of the week; he says that today is "my favourite day." In other words, Pooh lives in the now, not thinking about yesterday or next week. Pooh is content and happy with life's simple things, such as lying on the grass and looking at the clouds. As clever as Rabbit is, he cannot understand something truly unique like this.

The poem of "Cottleston Pie" explains the obvious (to some) that you can't put a square peg into a round hole in life. In other words, everything has its place and function, and many of us don't realise that WE are in the wrong place (whether it's your occupation, relationships or whatever).

We also have to realise what's there – the wise know their limitations; the foolish do not. Tigger knows no limitations of himself, even to the point of absurdity. The trouble with 'Tiggers' is that they want to do everything, which is very unhealthy (like the time he wanted to fly). Once we face and understand our limitations, we can learn from them. And once we find our limitations, then they can be our strengths.

Science likes to put labels on everything without saying much.
Curious: "Why do birds fly south (northern hemisphere) for the winter?"
Science: "Instinct."

This really means that we don't know - science has a habit of never really being able to say they don't know. The important thing here is that we don't NEED to know. We need to accept and work with things as they are. Pooh and Piglet find out this when they try to catch a Heffalump.

People are unusual as they are easily led away by what's right for them (what is right for you is another discussion for another day). Inner nature cannot be fooled, but most of us don't look or listen to it (most of us are probably in a hurry to make a decision). All of us have talent; all we need to do is use our weaknesses in a different direction. Regardless of what most of us think, there is no such thing as an ability that is too useless. It depends on what you do with it and what you "make it mean." As Lao-Tse pointed out - bad can lead to good. The reverse of this is also true.

In the story of the "Ugly Duckling", the ugly duckling stopped feeling ugly when she realised that she was a swan. How we look at things determines where our lives lead us most of the time. The wise are who they are; they work with what they have to do and what they have to do eventually.

"Tigger is all right really," said Piglet.
"Of course he is," said Christopher Robin.
"Everyone is really," said Pooh. "That's what I think, but I don't suppose I'm right."
"Of course you are," said Christopher Robin.

When we work with our inner nature with the natural laws, we operate on the law of minimal effort (Wu Wei). As the natural world works this way, there are no mistakes. Mistakes come from the over-thinking brain and from trying too hard. In other words, don't try to force things to happen; just let them happen.

"Just how do you do it, Pooh?"
"Do what?" asked Pooh.
"Become so effortless."
"I don't do much of anything," he said.
"But all those things of yours get done."
"They just sort of happen," he said.

Tao doesn't force things but lets things work in their own way, and what needs doing gets done. Things happen by themselves. When we work with Wu Wei, the round peg goes in the round hole and the square peg in the square hole. The ego tries to force the pegs into the wrong holes. Wu Wei does it without trying or thinking. Overthinking causes confusion. While working with Wu Wei, there are accidents, and while this may seem odd, things will work out. Don't try too hard and let things happen. Many of us try too hard because we want to control everything. Still, the reality is that we can't control very much at all – only ourselves.

Those who do things the Pooh way find this sort of thing happening all the time. This approach can be seen in the Taoist martial art T'ai Chi Ch'uan. The approach is to wear out the opponent by sending their energy back to them or via deflection. Never use force against force - remember, success does not come from hard work.

A Bisy Backson (BB) is a term to describe people who are always busy doing 'things' (like Owl). They strive to do more yet never really achieve anything of note and never stop to smell the roses of life. If you want to be healthy, relaxed and contented, watch people like Owl and do the opposite.

The ethics of religion, business and sciences would have us believe that we can only achieve success with these if we race around like a Bisy Backson. Never just looking at clouds and thinking how wonderful they are. Always saying "the end is just around the corner" is against the natural order of things, which leads to unhappiness and ordinary outcomes. The following is a meaningful conversation between the Author and Pooh:

"I say, Pooh, why aren't you busy?" I said.
"Because it's a nice day," said Pooh.
"Yes, but ..."
"Why ruin it?" he said.
"But you could be doing something important," I said.
"I am," said Pooh.

Sometimes we need to stop and appreciate nature and watch and listen to the noise of a forest. And not think about it too much. The classic Bisy Backson of life is the hamburger stand which says, "you don't count, hurry up".

In contrast, the Chinese tea-house says, "you're important; relax and enjoy yourself."

Unfortunately, in western society, we have many things that save us time like microwaves, mobile phones, computers and fast food. Still, we seem to have less time than ever before. For centuries, hard-working farmers and aristocrats in China died before 40, whereas Taoist people lived twice as long.

At this point, read the story of Li Chung Yun, who exemplifies the Taoist way of living. As you read this, you may start to question many things that "you think you have to do." On our journey toward whatever it is, enjoyment of the process is the most important thing, not the goal or destination that we strive for. It is the same thing as when just before Pooh eats his honey; some call it anticipation, but it is probably more awareness.

In the chapter "That Sort of Bear", there is another revealing story of the stone cutter, which you can discover for yourself.

To take control of our lives, we need to believe in ourselves and stop looking at what others do. Two famous examples of this are Buckminster Fuller and Thomas Edison. They both believed in their ideas and followed them through to completion despite their difficulties. As Pooh found out in the story of the North Pole - we need to utilise everything to accomplish what we want to do. These "things" are already there; we just need to find and use them.

In Taoism, Lao-Tse wrote, "from caring comes courage" from wisdom. Wisdom is not to be confused with knowledge, as knowledge doesn't have the caring aspect which sets them apart.

Pooh says that all of us can enjoy life and use who we are; some people just don't. Happiness comes from being appreciative of who we are; discontent causes the opposite.

Christopher Robin says, "what I like doing best is nothing. To have no thought and put forth no effort is the first step toward understanding the Tao. To go nowhere and do nothing is the first step toward finding peace in the Tao. To start from no point and follow no road is the first step towards reaching the Tao."

When Eeyore lost his tail, who found it for him? Clever Rabbit? No, he was too busy being clever. Scholarly Owl? No, he didn't even recognise it when he saw it. Know-it-all Eeyore? No, he didn't even realise it was missing. Pooh, with an empty mind, found it.

The trick here is not to be afraid of emptiness or loneliness, as emptiness is like fresh snow or a still pond. An overstuffed mind is unable to find things. Many of us are afraid of emptiness or loneliness.

We feel we should be doing something when sometimes the best thing we could be doing is nothing to clear our minds. Doing nothing is hard for many of us to do, yet most of our best ideas or thoughts come from when we are doing nothing. It seems as though we grow from childhood innocence, just enjoying what is in front of us, to an adult who plans everything but forgets to enjoy what is in front of them. There is much to be said about keeping our inner child rather than worrying about what might happen next week.

As Pooh has seen, a bear of very little brain, listening to the voice within us to tell us which way to go is somewhat better than thinking (as a brain does) about what we think may be real. In other words, going with your gut is usually better than over-thinking things.

It is a beautiful book, and the interactions between Pooh and the author are priceless yet straightforward. For that reason, I have left most of them out of my summary. This is a book anyone can read, and all the 'too busy' people should read. It is a book that you could read to your younger children. I would recommend reading the original Pooh series by A.A. Milne to enjoy Pooh and his friends for the little kids in your life.

CHAPTER ELEVEN

You are a Badass (Jen Sincero) 2013

This is one of the more "modern" books that I have covered here, and as soon as I started reading it, it felt like Jen was actually talking to me. Having heard Jen on a podcast previously certainly helped and was probably partly why my wife suggested that I read it. It is a book that doesn't mince words (which I like), and I wondered why I resonated with many of its aspects. Then I spotted the resources section at the back has a similar collection of books to mine as to where her inspiration comes from. This book is written and laid out differently from the others.

The introduction focuses on change and the difference between wanting and deciding. It deals with what we think we should (I hate the 's' word) and what we could be doing instead. Have you ever been to a motivational seminar, got yourself hyped up, but forgotten what it was about after a week? Well, I'm sure the author and most of us have. Money, or our thoughts of money, plays a significant role in our lives, but our fear of it determines our outcomes in life. To change for the better, think, "if I want to live a life I've never lived, I have to do things I've never done." Have a go - what have you got to lose?

"You are a victim of the rules you live by." (Jenny Holzer)

Our parents and society pass on their beliefs to us as children. We tend to accept these things as the truth, which of course, they are not (many of the things we think are the truth are just learned beliefs). The worst of this is that we are oblivious to the subconscious beliefs that run our lives. Our conscious mind thinks that it is in control, whereas it is in control of Jack. Our subconscious mind doesn't think at all, but it is the one that remains in control, and it takes everything that we hear at face value. In other words, it doesn't understand humour or sarcasm, so care needs to be taken with the words we use and our thoughts.

As a result, our subconscious develops our beliefs such as "money is the root of all evil." Making money and keeping it becomes virtually impossible with a thought such as this. These beliefs, which are out of alignment with what we want to achieve, develop the opposite outcome. Awareness of our limiting subconscious beliefs is critical in moving forward. At this point, consider your underlying beliefs and examine where they came from. We are all the same at birth; our environment determines many of our beliefs.

"If you want to find the secrets of the universe, think in terms of energy, frequency, and vibration"– Nikola Tesla.

This comment is so true, but maybe a little bit woo-woo for some at this stage. It refers to the fact that the universe is made up of source energy. All energy vibrates at a particular frequency, like when tuning your radio for a specific station. Our vibrations are critical, as like attracts like. The universe (or god, higher source, or whatever you believe in) will match whatever vibration you put out, and it cannot be fooled. To get what we want in life, we have to stay connected to source energy and hold the belief that everything is available to us. How we vibrate and what energy we show the universe will determine greatly how successful we are in life.

To quote Star Wars, "The force is always with you – always."

Chapter 3 discusses the importance of staying present with the now, not what happened before or what lies ahead. It goes on to say about clearing our minds of the meaningless crap we get ourselves into, and instead, act more like a young child or even a family pet. What has happened in the past is just that, nothing more, so don't attach any meaning to it. We all have plans for the future (human trait only) but don't live for tomorrow at the expense of enjoying what is in front of you. By over-thinking yesterday and tomorrow, we will never enjoy the best day of all – today. All things we want in life are in front of us; we have to slow down and become present to see them. Whether it be money or love, it is there.

Self-limiting beliefs or ego is described as the "big snooze" or BS (which I prefer). Our BS stands in the way of change or reaching our lofty goals. Our BS tries to keep us 'safe' by not venturing out to touch the sky. It comes from not trusting the inner you (which wants nothing less than to go for gold in life). It listens to the advice of others (well-meaning) who point out the dangers/futility of your potential move forward.

The common question is, "what happens when you fail?" You won't do anything if you adopt this attitude towards anything 'out of the normal'. It is the unknown that the BS is afraid of when the reality is that it could be fun. Making bold moves such as throwing away a high-paying job to live out your real desires requires courage, but the pay-off can be huge for us. The more important question is, "what life will you have if you don't chase your dreams?"

Our perceptions of ourselves play a massive part in what we are and do. The curious thing about perceptions is that our negative thoughts about ourselves require the same energy as positive ones. So why be negative when being positive in life is just as easy?

Chapter 6 talks about loving yourself, or my take is to stop judging ourselves and others. When we judge others, as many of us do, we also judge ourselves. It doesn't serve us at all. Negative thoughts about ourselves come from our environment, as we don't have these ideas when born (learned behaviour). When we are truly happy, and in love with ourselves, we are not influenced by the BS or our surroundings. We need to appreciate how special we are and verbalise it. Do things that we love; don't joke about any deficiencies we have; don't compare yourself with others; give yourself a break and love who you are when you need it. Get into a habit of telling yourself how special you are and that you love who you are. Do this first thing in the morning or while getting dressed, and make it a part of your day.

Imagine how liberating life would be if you didn't give a fig about what others thought of you. The reality is that the only things that you need to question are –

1. Is this what I want to be, do, have? (In this order, NOT have, do, be. An important distinction here). Work out who you want to be first, then think of what that person looks like, how they act, and what they do. Then be that person first.
2. Is this the way I want to go?
3. Is this going to hurt anyone?

Have you heard of the expression "nothing ventured/nothing gained?" We are only responsible for what we say and do - what others think of us is on them. We sometimes have to get out of our comfort zone to achieve what we want (like writing a book when it is easier to watch Netflix at night after work). We will never do anything if we worry about what others think of what we want to do. Watch a football game with a mate that supports "the other team" to see how different our perceptions can be.

Chapter 8 focuses on finding your purpose in life - and this is the secret to happiness. Sometimes we have to look from afar to see ourselves. Once we understand ourselves and use our unique abilities (which we all have), the sky can be the limit. The first step (trusting your gut) is huge, but it has to be taken. Workaround what interests you, and you will follow your dreams and aspirations. Most importantly, love yourself (a very common theme in this book).

Meditation is crucial as it raises our frequency. It relaxes us, relieves stress, removes the monkey chatter in our brains and helps us to love ourselves. Tips for meditation, which you need to read, are in chapter 10.

Chapter 11 refers to the enormous power that words and thoughts have. "I think, therefore, I can." Combining our thoughts with the source energy of the universe is how we succeed. Most importantly, our thoughts have to change before anything else to achieve. "Ask, and you shall receive" (The Bible). After asking, act as if you have already succeeded and surround yourself with like-minded positive people. You won't get there by surrounding yourself with "Debbie-Downers."

As we become older, we tend to lose the recklessness of youth. This can be a good thing. However, it can also stop us from achieving. We are all only here for a "short" time, so we need to enjoy our journey. Life needs to be an adventure, so grab it by the balls and do what you love.

"It is better to give than to receive", and really to receive, you have to give without any expectations as these never help us. Give money, time, and even smiles frequently and be surprised at how good you feel. This, in turn, raises your frequency leading you to be open to positive outcomes.

"When you are grateful, fear disappears, and abundance appears" (Anthony Robbins).

It is so true. Be truly grateful for everything in your life. Jen talks about people not saying "thank you" after receiving something. After all, thank you is only two words, so how powerful can it be? Even when life takes a supposed "nasty" turn, there is always something to be thankful for. Being grateful raises your energy and increases the chance of possibilities for you. And staying in this state boosts your energy to the point that your thoughts can become a reality. Many people may call this faith or be grateful for imaginary things, but it works whatever you call it.

The art of forgiveness (similar to gratitude in some ways) is the way to your freedom. Forgiving isn't about being nice to another person; it's about being nice to yourself. Being happy is so much better than being "right." Being "right" is more about your ego than anything else. Apart from exams, when has "being right" in any relationship given you a positive result?

In chapter 16, Jen talks about her life-changing trip to India. There are important lessons that she learnt here from a different culture to her own.

Chapter 17, in my opinion, is the most important in terms of our ability to separate beliefs from facts. "What you choose to focus on becomes your reality." Where we are in life is determined by how we choose to perceive our reality. In other words, our stories can define us. Only a tiny percentage of what we think are facts are facts and are just our beliefs or opinions. We have to become aware of our stories and what we gain by having them. If your stories about this aren't doing you any favours, you are better off without them. Stop leaning on what makes problems more significant than the greatness of Ben Hur and change your routine to lead to new possibilities.

Fear, you say, "I'm not fearful." If procrastination and perfectionism are part of your life, then so is fear. Procrastination comes from perfectionism (anything but), which comes from fear. Many people fear being disliked or rejected, which prevents them from reaching their potential. Jen talks about fear in Chapter 20 and how many of us have made fear a habit. Fear is usually just about the unknown future. If we live our lives in the present and be aware of our surroundings without living in it, fear loses control. Stay in the NOW and think less.

Our surroundings reflect who we are, what we do and how we think. Look in the mirror to see and understand the reality you have created for yourself. Most importantly, take ownership of where you are in life due to who you have been.

This is all on us. "No one can make you feel inferior without your consent" – Eleanor Roosevelt.

At the end of the day, it's not about those who criticise us; it is about you believing you're worthy of being loved and seen for who you are. "It's about respecting yourself instead of catering to your insecure need to be liked." It is far easier if we have no attachment to "being liked" while being confident in ourselves. Don't look to "being liked" by everyone; instead, like your reasons for being who you are and what you can achieve.

One of the book's key points is when Jen talks about what drives you nuts about people. These things can result in us getting really worked up. The reality is that things we don't like are usually reflections of ourselves. What we don't like about others, we do ourselves. Should we be bothered by this? Nope. Stay away from people you perceive as painful; spend time with people you love. Ask yourself, 'what do I get by feeling this way?'

"So often we pretend we've made a decision when what we've done is signed up to try until it gets too uncomfortable." Decisions lead to success, which doesn't come easy to most of us, and initial failure is very common. Ask Jordan, Spielberg, Edison, Honda or Beethoven about failure - they have all experienced failure at some point. But the only absolute failure is quitting. To succeed, we have to want it BAD. Then decide what to do, for indecision is torture. Once you decide, do not second-guess yourself, and lastly, don't quit. As my wife would say, "no backtracking", which has become a mantra for us. It is not scary at all.

Chapter 24 dives into the elephant in the room – money. Jen describes her thoughts about buying a car or car that she loves. Most of us can relate to this – using "our heads" to buy a functional car or using our "hearts" to buy a really "cool" car. But money isn't really about money; it is more about the energy around it. When we operate on high frequency (loving money and thinking in abundance), it manifests in our lives. We have to have a positive relationship with money to attract abundance. No fear or loathing works here. Beliefs are crucial to it all, and a belief in the abundance of wealth around us is critical. There are five steps to wealth creation highlighted, and I would suggest reading them as they hold an important key to the door to success.

An interesting statistic in chapter 26 is that only five per cent of people who do a course or seminar do something with it. Most of us like the idea of change but don't like feeling uncomfortable making something happen. As Jen intimates, most people will read a self-help book and say, "this is an awesome book", and recommend it to their friends while actioning very little of it. If you want something different, then feeling uncomfortable is part of it.

The central theme is to keep the faith even when everything is on the line throughout the stories. Jen explains her nomadic life here while going with the universe's flow while also (she is human) having moments of self-doubt. At the end of the book, Jen shares nine steps for basing your future on (good idea to follow). Just be yourself, believe in yourself, and your dreams and the world could be yours.

"You are a Badass" is a more modern way of looking at more than a hundred years old concepts. This book focuses on enjoying life while learning concepts that will make your life easier. The way Jen writes is very conversational, and it is as if she is speaking in front of you. But as Jen says, you have to make the first move and buy this book. Then the rest is up to you.

CHAPTER TWELVE

The 7 Habits of Highly Effective People (Stephen R Covey 1989)

The "7 Habits" is the psychology handbook of its time and, for that matter, any time. Covey's principles can be applied in every aspect of your life. The highlighted habits ask questions of ourselves and one's impact on others in our lives. This book changed the way that people think about others. Our current generation should read it with regard to doing things without thinking and the subsequent consequences. Covey writes with a blend of wisdom, compassion and practical experiences. In a way, this book has become a reference book regarding personal interactions. The world would be a better place if every adult would read this book at least once. Personally, this book was probably the first self-help book I read, and it helped put my wife and me on a wonderful journey in life.

The first part of the book is titled Inside-Out. The nuts and bolts of this are that if we want to change a situation that we are in, we first have to change ourselves. And this only comes from changing our perceptions. Many of us use something that Covey calls the personality ethic. This is where we function from the point of public image and community attitudes/behaviours - looking at an issue from how we see things.

Outside-In. Instead of trying to change others, focus your efforts on your motives and perceptions. If we try to get others to do as we want without getting our stuff together, we won't be successful in the long term. It's like cramming for an exam – you might pass the subject; however, the knowledge won't stay with you.

Relationships require long-term integrity and character and without which they will fail. Who or what we are, reveals far more about ourselves than what we say or do. We all know someone we trust absolutely and those we don't. We need to make a paradigm shift, and this is more of a model, theory or reference. It is like having access to Google maps, without which you will get lost no matter how hard you work to find your way. We have maps in our heads of how things are and other maps of how things should be, which translates to us making many assumptions. The way we see things determines what we think and how we behave. Look at the picture on page 25 (of a woman - old or beautiful) and follow the steps to see the meaning. Our assumptions can lead us to places that we don't want to go to by making them into facts which they aren't.

It is incredible how conditioning affects our perceptions and paradigms and demonstrates where our attitudes and behaviours come from. Even if we feel we are being objective about our opinions, others may have the opposite view depending on where they are coming from. We are not objective as we see the world as we are programmed. Having awareness about our paradigms is essential as we need to challenge these more so to obtain a far more objective view of the world. Many of us receive a shift when faced with a life-threatening crisis and see the world in a different light.

As we develop our character, our paradigm shifts, and we see the world differently. It may happen quickly or very slowly. Principles such as fairness, integrity, honesty, service and human dignity act as clear guidelines for people on the journey to successful relationships. Relationships are built on these principles, and similar to building wealth, there is no quick fix that will work long term. Also, it has to be said; that there are multiple different ways of reaching success as our journey is unique to ourselves.

As children, we have to learn how to walk, run and throw a ball. At the same time, we also have to develop emotional characteristics. It is where many of us fall as adults as we are usually looking for an easy way. Shortcuts rarely work and typically lead to disappointment and general frustration. For any relationship to work, we must learn how to listen. This requires patience and the desire to understand – sounds easy, doesn't it. But, it is far easier to advise without listening "to." These problems also occur in the business world, where leaders try to buy a new "culture" without doing the heavy lifting.

There is a time to teach and not to teach with any relationship. When emotions get heated, and there is "some skin in the game", satisfactory decisions are rarely made.

The way everybody sees problems usually contributes to the actual situation. We all come from different positions in life and have different ways of looking at everything. We need to place ourselves in the other person's position to see what they see.

Einstein said, "the significant problems we face cannot be solved at the same level of thinking we were at when we created them."

So an approach is required that works from our inner selves outwards - starting with our paradigms, characteristics, and motives for doing what we do. In other words, we have to be true to ourselves first before going on to improve our relationships. This process sees us working on ourselves first to be the best version we can be. We can't help others until we have fixed ourselves first.

Aristotle says, "we are what we repeatedly do. Excellence then is not an act, but a habit."

Meaning - we are our habits. Habits combine knowledge, skill and desire and creating a new habit involves all three. Knowing what to do isn't enough; we also need to have the skill and desire to do so.

Life by nature is interdependent. When we are born, we are dependent on others for just about everything. As we mature, we become more independent and branch out further. The goal is to become interdependent where we can work in harmony with our environments and create possible greatness. Interdependence is a choice that only independent people can make. Dependent people haven't the character to achieve this by themselves. This is because they are dependent on others for most things and are also reliant on their environment.

With "The 7 Habits", it is best to do the exercises at the end of every chapter to get the most out of it. Please read the book to discuss it with someone close to you soon after. This makes it far easier to remember the concepts and really understand them. We will find ourselves thinking less about what others think and find life more enjoyable by working on ourselves. Remember, "Rome wasn't built in a day", so be fair to yourself as you journey through the "7 Habits."

Habit 1 Be Proactive

The critical word here is 'be'. In life, our feelings and thoughts are not who we are. We are merely the thinker of these things. It is essential to recognise how we see ourselves and others. Without this, we cannot understand others and where they are coming from.

We can choose for ourselves that our environment, genetics and upbringing determine who we are as people. This way of thinking provides excuses for not reaching our potential. Or we can choose a powerful way of thinking to decide who we are and how external circumstances play only a small part in our lives. It is a choice. If we live the first way, then our lives will be limited, and who wants that?

We can choose our response to what is happening in the world. If we decide to react to what is around us, we are reactive and will either be happy or sad depending on our environment. More than likely, we will be sad if we think this way as our various forms of media are rarely positive about our world. If we are proactive, the environment makes little difference to how we feel.

Eleanor Roosevelt observed, "no one can hurt you without your consent."

Gandhi says, "they cannot take away our self-respect if we do not give it to them."

Both statements are powerful and true. Who we are now is because of the choices that we have made. Own this sentence.

We have all seen cases of people in very difficult circumstances, like Steven Hawking. They rise above the normal and achieve greatness. Our response to what happens to us is really what can make or break us. Taking the initiative and being proactive leads to success instead of waiting for things to happen. The result is like the difference between night and day. By doing so, we are facing our reality and not facing our reality is like putting your head in the sand.

The words that we use in general life say a lot about us. They are 'only' words, but these words will go a long way in determining what life you lead. Language can either be reactive (I can't, I have to do that, that makes me so mad or if only etc.) or proactive (I choose, I will, I control my own feelings etc.). Using reactive language means living a life of blame for all things external to where we are.

Think of your life as having two circles, an inner circle which is our circle of influence and an outer circle, which is our circle of concern.

Proactive people have a large influence circle because of their positive energy, making their outer circle of concern smaller.

Changing our habits, words, and how we see the world gives us control over our experiences. Reactive people have a much smaller inner circle of influence with a large outer circle (generated by negative energy) of concern. Which model would you prefer?

Others can see proactive people as pushy or insensitive, but this isn't the case. Proactive people tend to be innovative and know what is needed when it is required. Gandhi is an excellent example of someone who changed India's future without having any real external power.

The circle of concern is filled with "if only if I had more time, I'd be happy when…", whereas the circle of influence is filled with "be wise, be happy, be patient." It is always far easier to blame others or conditions for the life that we lead. Being responsible for one's situation is more difficult but far more rewarding as you take control of your life. We can only really control ourselves, so this is what we need to concentrate on. For example, how do we be happy? The answer is to smile at life and decide that you will be happy. Too easy, you say? Try doing it and see what difference it makes.

People who live their lives in regret of past mistakes are expanding their circle of concern. We can't change the past, so why dwell about it. Sometimes it would be easier to be like Dory from "Finding Nemo", who doesn't remember what she did five minutes ago. Life would be far simpler that way. The only problem with being Dory is that you won't learn from your mistakes.

The word commitment is within the circle of influence, which is important for maintaining our self-integrity. The size of the commitment doesn't matter just as long as we stay in integrity with it.

At the end of this chapter, there is a 30-day test that I would suggest that you do to honour your commitment to being proactive.

Habit 2 Begin With The End in Mind

By having a clear mental image of the end of your life, you will have a clear vision of what you want to achieve in life and how you want to do it. Then it is easier to stay aligned each day with our end goal. Having the end goal in mind makes it easier not to get distracted by the things that don't serve us. People are easily sidetracked by many things in life, which makes us busier but not very effective. Most of us are quite good at being busy but not really going anywhere. We can all put up our hands to say I am guilty of this.

To Peter Drucker and Warren Bennis, "Management is doing things right; Leadership is doing the right things."

Imagine you and a friend are in the "Amazing Race", and one of you is driving and the other is navigating. The navigating person says, "we are going in the wrong direction". At the same time, the driver (management) is quite happy driving as they are making "good time." Making "good time" won't help if you are going in the wrong direction. Our effectiveness doesn't depend on our effort but comes from being on the right road to success. To be proactive in life, we need to use our imagination and conscience. In life, there are many paths in front of us that we can take and discover - we just have to choose the best path for us. And just because we have decided to choose a particular path doesn't mean we have to stay on it. A good example of this is the roads taken by Anwar Sadat, which ended in unlikely peace accords. It is only possible through our self-awareness leading to our imagination and conscience.

A personal mission statement is powerful as it focuses on who/what you want to be and the actions that you will take to get there. This then becomes the basis for all of our decisions regardless of our lives' circumstances and emotional stuff. To do this, we must start at the centre of our circle of influence which is the source of our security, guidance, wisdom and power.

As we are human and have enormous potential, factors (different centres) can derail our effectiveness. These factors are spousal, family, money, work, possession, pleasure, friend/enemy, church and self. These factors have advantages, but they also have downsides, which we need to detach ourselves from. Self can lead to selfishness, but on the other hand, the development of oneself can improve our ability to serve the world and change the lives of many. To understand this point more, read the chapter yourself.

Having a centre based on principles (which don't react to what's going on in our world) is where the real personal power comes from. This certainly creates a fundamental paradigm for effective living. With this, you will see things differently and, as a result, think differently. That way, we can see the world more clearly and relate more easily to our environment. This is, again, where a mission statement is so powerful.

Visualisation and affirmations are habits that can achieve greatness. Most high achievers in sport or business visualise. They start at the end. Effective goals focus on results rather than just doing. Goals give us the information on getting to where we want to be and tell us when we have got there.

Like personal mission statements, family and organisational mission statements are like gold. The major difference here is that it is a combination of different thoughts and ideas, which is the basis of power. Staff and family members should all contribute equally to the statement as this gives them ownership of it. If management, parents, or leaders do this, the followers won't follow with their hearts.

Habit 3 Put First Things First

"Things which matter most must never be at the mercy of things which matter least" – Goethe.

Habit 3 is really about practicing self-management. Our independent will makes it possible to make decisions and choices and then act on them. How effective we are at this is determined by our self-integrity to ourselves. Without self-integrity, success in life will be just a dream. This involves doing things we don't necessarily want to do but need to do to succeed. It is one of the differences between the successful people in life and the others who do all the "stuff" they like doing.

Time management is necessary here, as we have to organise and follow through around our priorities. We have to determine what activities are urgent/non-urgent and important/non-important. The more successful people tend not to see problems as problems but to see them more as opportunities and in terms of thinking preventively.

Much of the success here comes from being able to say 'no' respectively to things that can take up your time but are inconsistent with where you want to go. We still do things for others that don't help us, but we have to be selective about our choices. Whatever our choices, we must keep the end in mind, which comes from internalising that habit. How we spend our time comes from how we view our priorities. If our priorities align with our personal mission statement, decisions become easier.

Planning our lives from a centre of sound principles is key to becoming better organised - but just planning our lives is not the solution. The best planning includes the following:

1. Principle centred approach
2. Conscience directed
3. Defines your unique mission

4. Gives you balance
5. It provides greater context to yourself, keeping you aligned with your values.

The part missing from all this is delegation, which is essential in achieving anything. Sometimes we have to learn how to release our control over everything in our lives. Delegation allows others to do some of your heavy lifting instead of you doing it all. Many people have trouble with this, as they want to "control" everything. We can never do this effectively by ourselves.

Our relationships with people are determined by many seemingly small things that add up over time. This is what is known as an Emotional Bank Account. It is affected by the following:

1. Understanding each other can simply be done by bonding and showing an interest.
2. Doing the little things that may seem unimportant to you can be huge to others.
3. Keeping your commitments.
4. Clarifying expectations. It is amazing how two people can hear the same thing but have different interpretations, causing problems.
5. Having personal integrity.
6. Being sincere when you stuff up.

Habit 4 Think Win/Win

Win/Win is one of the six paradigms of human interaction. It works the best while working from the basis of abundance. There is plenty for everyone - it doesn't have to be dog eat dog. It means that someone's success doesn't have to come at the expense of somebody else's. In fact, in life, if Win/Win is not going to work out, then No Deal is the next best thing. This is a winning strategy, particularly in a negotiation. Life doesn't have to be a competition. Win/Win involves co-operation, respecting others and working along/with others to achieve an outcome where everyone can benefit. It isn't like playing Monopoly – not that there is anything wrong with that. Think of the positive energy surrounding transactions where both sides can be happy with the outcome.

Character traits such as high integrity, maturity and a feeling of abundance are all hallmarks of the Win/Win. The abundance mentality means there is enough for everyone and that our imagination only limits the rewards. "The Treaty of Versailles" at the end of WW1 is a typical example of a win/lose transaction that laid the platform for WW2. In this situation, there was a feeling of wanting "Germany to pay for what they have done." The problem with our emotions is that sometimes they get in the way of making a more logical agreement/solution. Relationships through genuine courtesy, respect and appreciation of others and their thoughts are essential for Win/Win to work. Having agreements where there is a common objective also helps.

As with anything in life, a Win/Win strategy works consistently when it becomes a habit of ours. Developing habits of performance and attitude (in any field) requires a clear picture of the end goal. This means focusing on the results, not so much on the method used to get there. When teams of people are "on board" with where they are going, individuals become more accountable for their work and improve. Managers/coaches need to lead by example, and others will follow. Systems that motivate and encourage staff need to be implemented. Good systems are the blueprint for organisations to achieve Win/Win effectively.

Habit 5 Seek First to Understand, Then to be Understood

The subtle art of actively listening and understanding what others are saying BEFORE you talk is a great skill. The people who get this are great communicators, whereas most of us don't have the patience for it. Most of us want to be understood, but we don't really understand what is happening inside the person we are talking to. Most of us are either "listening" so that we only get half of what is going on, or we are too busy thinking about how we should respond. Put your hand up if you have ever been guilty of this. I know I have.

Real listening (empathic) involves getting inside another person and seeing things as they do or feel. This is real communication instead of imprinting our beliefs and opinions on others. And people do notice the difference. Imagine what you could do if you could do this. As we learn to understand others, we will become amazed at the flow of knowledge between two people. Sometimes we just need to listen and not talk. The key to all of this is your sincerity, without which none of this works. Be sincere with yourself and others, and remember that everyone wants to be understood above most things. Once we understand others, we can present our ideas without trying to "win" a conversation. The more we appreciate others, the more "winning" becomes less important.

Habit 6 Synergize

Synergy is like the sum of the previous five habits that end up as our greatest power. Synergy creates the most exciting advances (and most scary) possible for us. It is found everywhere in nature, much like the interaction of plants in a forest. It can also be found in a business where two similar businesses co-exist next to each other, helping each other grow. Many of us are still using win-lose defensive strategies and will never experience the opportunity of synergy. Synergy becomes most influential and exciting in aligned groups as spirits are lifted, and creative ideas emerge easily in this situation. This way, the result is far greater than the sum of all individuals (inputs) put together.

It all comes down to how we think and feel—the more people we have in synergy, the more outstanding the achievement. We must value our differences in beliefs and opinions as in a dispute; both sides can be right. Consider the ink-blot test where we are asked what each blot reminds us of; there will be many different answers, and they are all correct.

Habit 7 Sharpen the Saw

This habit is all about improving your greatest asset – you. This is done in four ways – physical, mental, spiritual and emotional. The physical way is to look after our bodies with the proper nutrition, exercise and balance in our lives. Spiritual involves looking after what is important to you, which can mean many different things to many other people. Mental involves us using our minds towards things that can improve us. Spending hours on social media or surfing the net for something to do may be fun, but you won't achieve much by doing this. Instead, expand your education by reading or taking courses that can improve your life. Our emotions improve our being. When we are at peace with ourselves, our emotions will be balanced, and life will become easier.

Who we are, how we are, and how we conduct ourselves with others are critical for our development. When our emotions are not balanced, we tend to overreact to even the smallest things in our lives. Treat others as you would like to be treated yourself. Smile and believe in others, and your actions will be repeated back to you.

As we become more self-aware, then things will fall in place naturally. As with most things in life – don't force things to happen; just let them happen. Making the habits part of your life is a recipe for success. Steven Covey's 7 Habits is like a guide to life and a 'how to' book about interacting with people. Two 'rules' at the back of the book can be key here. Firstly, not to judge others for what they do. This is important as judging others means that we are judging ourselves, and there is nothing to be gained by doing this. The second is not to force things when they are not ready to be moved. This can be anytime doing anything. And above all, value your integrity, for you have very little without this. Do the exercises in the book and make the seven habits part of your life.

CHAPTER THIRTEEN

Awareness (1990) Anthony De Mello

Anthony De Mello was an Indian Jesuit priest, and he was known for being a spiritual teacher and writer. He wrote several books about spirituality. He was recognised for his stories from the traditions of the East and the West. He transitioned from our world in 1987. This book is more of a guide to help us understand the importance of awareness to understand ourselves and the world we live in. Understanding ourselves will help with most of the issues we face in our lives, as most of the answers to many of our questions lie within us.

Are you awake? Yes, you say - but more than likely, you are asleep most of the time. For most of us, we are more awake when we are sleeping. How you live your life depends on your thoughts and prejudices. Most of us want things like happiness, but only on our terms. We have to stop thinking this way to awaken, and then we will enjoy freedom, peace or spirituality (or all three).

When you renounce something, you are stuck to it forever. When you fight something, you become tied to it forever - and as long as you're fighting it, you give it power (P16). In other words, we attract whatever we are thinking. If you are constantly thinking of the negatives in the world/your life, that is the energy you are attracting. Aspire for what you want in life, not what you don't want. There is a huge difference.

Are you listening? Or, as most people, waiting to hear something that confirms your beliefs? Or are you consciously listening so that you can discover something new and exciting (P17)? Most of us are doing the former. You might say not me - but ask yourself which news you listen to or read? Unfortunately, most news services (TV, radio, newspapers, internet) are biased one way or the other. You "like" what you watch or read because it confirms your beliefs. Again, if you disagree with this, ask yourself TRUTHFULLY why you like it. If you want to know what is going on in the world, watch what you DON'T like. Even better, please don't get too involved personally in any of it. The reality is that new, good news is quickly rejected as we don't like change.

The pages of charity (19-26) discuss the selfishness of helping others and why what appears to be charity is enlightened self-interest. De Mello challenges our thoughts of feeling good about ourselves for helping others. He also challenges the idea that religion isn't necessarily connected with spirituality. This chapter may upset some people, but its meaning is true, and we need to hear it.

The world is abundant (p26), but they can't see it as most people are asleep (not aware). Sometimes we have to listen (and accept) the ideas of others who challenge our beliefs. This isn't easy as emotions always make things more challenging. Real listening is the most challenging thing to do as it means that we have to lose control (which we all cherish), which then leads to fear - and this never feels good.

To wake up (and become more aware on p32), you will see through and learn not to expect anything from anyone. Expectations cause so much grief for all of us. Once you have managed this, you will never be disappointed or disillusioned with people, leading to happiness.

You want to hope for something better in life, but we forget that we have it all right now (P35). Be grateful for everything in your life, from the water you drink to your friends and family. The more things you can find to be grateful for, the happier you will be. Concentrate on the now, not the future or the past. This is one of the most important phrases you will read but probably not realise.

Observing ourselves is critical (P36). This means not to personalise any of your feelings. You need to look at things without any attachment and become a passive, detached observer. Above all else, don't fix anything. Just watch and observe. Sometimes looking in the mirror is the most challenging thing to do. Through observation and understanding, you can change yourself to the point where you don't interfere or judge others. By doing this, the change to living a life of awareness will happen relatively effortlessly. Effortlessly doesn't mean easy.

To know who you are is the foundation of everything (P45). Self-observation is watching whatever is happening around you (or in you) as if it is happening to somebody else. This can be scary and painful, and understand that your thoughts are just a mixture of our experiences.

Negative feelings are an illusion - in that you do not see reality (P51). When you have a negative feeling, the one who has to change is YOU. Negative feelings are a very human trait, as, without them, we would be far more effective. As we move into action about "righting a wrong", it is important that you see things with detachment. Negative emotions stop this.

The problem with being dependent on others emotionally is that our happiness comes from others. This, in turn, can lead to fear. Perfect love comes without fear, meaning happiness is not connected to dependency. With no dependence or demands on others, there are no expectations placed on others. Awareness is about not needing others psychologically or emotionally, which leads to your happiness. Lack of expectation leads to a cure for loneliness. A relationship does not cure loneliness; it is cured by reality. This all adds to happiness being a state of mind and comes from within you.

How can you have happiness (P56)? How can you have awareness? If you are fortunate, these things can come easily, and you will fear nobody and fear nothing relatively quickly. For most of us, though, awareness will improve in smaller stages. Still, with perseverance, small differences will be apparent within weeks. Making all of these your daily habits makes things easier and more effective. With happiness, we understand what it means to be alone, leave everyone freely, be free yourself, be special to nobody, and love everyone.

We think love is just desire, control and possessiveness (P61). Manipulation, fear and anxiety are not love. Happiness doesn't come when you achieve something or rid yourself of ills. (You may get a short-term sugar hit from achievement or winning the lotto, but it won't be long lasting). Happiness comes from being in the NOW, and you have everything you need to achieve this. This is available to anyone who listens.

Ignorance and fear are where evil and violence come from. Anger comes from fear meaning angry people are afraid. Love and fear are opposites.

"Fear and anger lead to the dark side" – Yoda.

Awareness, love, spirituality and real freedom are the same things. Once you can see something happening to yourself as if it is happening to someone else, you will understand what awareness is. Sometimes we have almost to detach ourselves from emotions to achieve this.

Loving, not praying in a religious mode, is spirituality, and when you have this, you have God. Sometimes, the sacrament and the sabbath become more important than Christ and life itself with organised religion. This is not the way it was meant to be. Being aware of what you are saying, doing, thinking and acting is most important, and without this, life is not worth living. In other words, don't just go to "church" on the weekend while not being aware of what you are doing for the other six days of the week.

It is not human to be unaware of yourself and your surroundings. Many people go through life with fixed ideas and never really change. We can miss things that happen right in front of us without awareness. With awareness, you control what is in front of you. Whereas without, what is in front of you has control.

"Don't seek the truth; just drop your opinions" (P73). Most of what we think is the truth is just our opinions or beliefs. So why get involved in an argument about them? Winning an argument is just about ego and nothing else.

What does success mean? The reality is that it doesn't mean much at all. The so-called "normal" success of a job or business venture means very little. Being aware makes you successful, so stop identifying yourself as your profession. This can come and go (particularly in the 21st century, where many people have multiple professions in their lifetime). To be unaffected by success means that no criticism can hurt you. Again, criticisms come and go. I think of the song from the movie "Frozen" where they sing "Let it go" when thinking of how not to make things mean something.

People or things cannot make us happy. Happiness is our factory setting, which can best be witnessed in babies and little children. We lose this setting by becoming involved in stupidity, which is much of our culture (supposedly "growing up"). Many of us may feel that what we are getting ourselves involved in isn't stupid. But ask yourself truthfully, "am I doing this because of my beliefs or ego and what real change has happened from thinking this way?" Real happiness comes from ourselves when we see that life is easy and delightful. Greed, ambitions and cravings take happiness away.

4 Steps to Wisdom (P78):

1. Get in touch with your negative feelings.

2. Understand that negative feelings are within you, not the real world. Problems exist only in our minds.
3. Never identify with the negative feelings. Don't say, "I am depressed." Don't feel that you have to do anything to be happy.
4. How do we change things? We change 'things' by changing our thoughts and feeling good.

As you awaken and understand, you will see that the world makes sense (P84). Over the following two pages is a powerful story about this, and you will need to buy the book to read it. Life is a mystery, and thinking cannot make sense of it. As you awaken, you will realise that you are the problem. In trying to fix things in the world (while asleep), we substitute one injustice for another. As we awaken, you will know what to do or what not to do. Everything becomes beautiful when we change. Remember, we see things and people not as they are but as we are. We have our filters for everything, and we put people in "boxes" so that we can "understand" them. By awakening, you understand that you don't have to make good things happen; they just happen (don't try to force things to happen). As you change, you will find that others will change around you and see them in a completely different light. Change won't happen while you are judging people.

Understanding, not doing, will change us (P90). Sometimes in life, it is much better to smell the roses rather than to pick the roses and give them to your partner. Competition is just a way to 'enjoy' a victory over someone else and, as such, takes away the pure enjoyment of doing something that you love. Don't let others try to tell you what to do – follow your inclinations (your gut) and tastes.

It is okay to say no to others, as long as you don't tell others to do what you think is right. It is not selfish to live your life as you see fit (P93). Once you drop your expectations and attachments, you will become more at peace with everybody and everything. This is because you lose the fear of being hurt or not being liked. Expectations and demands are there for society to function, for law and order, not to make leaders feel good.

A powerful proverb in the East is that "Those who know, do not say; those who say, do not know." Ponder that before saying something "smart" (P99).

In many forms of literature, spiritual and religious is the saying about losing yourself to find yourself (P103). You are never so full of yourself as when you're in pain - when you are depressed, you are heavily centred on yourself. Happiness comes from being ready to forget yourself and releasing yourself from yourself. Imagine you have a toothache and how conscious you are of your tooth, but you are not aware of your teeth when you don't have a toothache. To find ourselves, we need to get to the point where we can look at ourselves from the outside looking in (P106).

Unfortunately, we don't grow from pleasant experiences; we grow from painful ones. Negative feelings help gain awareness and understanding. Every time you are unhappy, you have added a negative emotion to reality. Suppression of desire leads to a lack of energy, and energy is important and needed. Desire needs to be understood more than it needs to be fulfilled.

To really live, you have to go with the flow. To be constantly happy, you must change frequently, listen to what life is, and don't look back. To be loved and respected is a natural urge, but dropping this urge will lead to happiness. You can become happy not being loved or desired/attractive to someone. You become happy with contact with reality (P113).

External events can't hurt us unless we give power to them. We are not what people call us. When we are truly happy and aware, our environment and circumstances won't define us. Don't look into the future, as this creates anxiety. Also, don't look into the past. This is purely something that has happened with no meaning to how you are now. Live in the present and enjoy it.

Emotions, likes, dislikes, preferences and attractions get into how we see people. So we have to be aware of our prejudices. As a result, we tend to 'see' (awakening) our partners AFTER we marry them. Ideas and words splinter the vision or experience of reality, and they can only act as pointers to reality. To know reality, you have to know beyond knowing. Awareness is watching and observing what is going on about you. The filters, as described above, distorts our perceptions of reality.

Happiness doesn't come from the success of acceptance, approval or applause. Remember, we need not be defined by what other people think of us - only our thoughts are truly important. Understanding that happiness comes from within you, not from external things, is one of the most important themes of the entire book. Having things, success, a partner, or fame can cause moments of joy, but this is fleeting. This doesn't mean that these things are bad; what is wrong is our attachment to these things. True happiness comes from the appreciation/gratitude of the external world without the attachment that many crave.

It is no surprise that anger and love also come from within. When people become angry at something or someone, the anger comes from themselves, not from external happenings. No one can make you angry – YOU do this to YOURSELF. When people say, "someone has triggered me", it means "I have triggered myself." Once we truly realise this, then we have true personal power. Being objective about external happenings is a sign of awareness. Anger is not. Knowledge and awareness are separate. Evil cannot exist with those who are aware, but one can do evil with knowledge or information. Jesus said, "Father, forgive them, for they know not what they do."

The harder that we try to change, the worse it can get. The more you resist something, the greater power you give to it actually to attract it. Don't try to force anything. An example of this is a person trying to lose weight, saying, "I will lose 30 Kilos and not eat chocolate anymore." This is attracting weight and chocolate. Better to think of your future self as having lost the weight and who is someone who doesn't eat chocolate. The differences can be subtle initially, but the end result certainly won't be.

Realise that life has no meaning. Sometimes it is better not to over-think everything and just accept what is. Perceive life as a mystery without expectations, and then life will make sense.

Loneliness is when you are missing people; aloneness is when you are enjoying yourself. Enjoy yourself first; then, it doesn't matter who is around you. Awareness is about not "wanting" anything; awareness is something you do or do not ("there is no try" – Yoda, Star Wars).

All evil comes from ignorance (P150). Awakening is the death of your belief in injustice and tragedy. Don't ask the world to change; just change oneself (the only thing we have any control over anyway). Changing others or things is just really doing something for your beliefs to make yourself feel better. Understanding and insight of ourselves are fundamental to our ability to self-change. Pushing things or using force is not the answer. We have to allow change to happen. As you begin to observe yourself, you will notice the difference. You will have to deal with self-condemnation, self-hatred and dissatisfaction with yourself—all of the self-sabotage things that complicate life.

Wisdom comes from the mind being unobstructed by dropping barriers that we have put up through our concepts (beliefs) and conditioning. Plato said, “One cannot make a slave of a free person, for a free person is free even in prison.” (Nelson Mandela would have thought like this during his many years of prison). Freedom comes from within, not from external forces.

Enjoying life and your senses is great nourishment for us. Simple things like good food, water, an interesting book or a good healthy discussion help us thrive in not wanting ‘things’. Always be grateful for these things in your life, and give your thanks for these basics. Most of us don’t want these simple things. It is like going to Niagara Falls and taking a thousand photos and posting on social media to show how “amazing” you are against just appreciating the beauty and watching the water flow.

Knowledge and awareness are two separate things. We can know something that could kill us (e.g., smoking), but it is only when we become aware that we will stop doing it.

Living comes from truly accepting death. Once we accept death wholly, our worries, anxiety, and concerns become less so, leading to awareness and true enjoyment. In other words, to truly enjoy life, we have to accept that death is just another chapter.

The ability to love comes from true independence. Once you depend on nobody for anything, your awareness will improve. Going into nature, away from crowds and being silent, helps. Freedom comes from this. It is not from a lack of religion in the ordinary sense of the word that the world is suffering – it is from a lack of love and awareness.

The ‘aha” experience brings us insight which leads to change. This happens when we are open to it. So much of our time is spent doing "important" things that we fail to see what is truly around us. Feelings are within us, not from the external. The feeling you get with nature, when you are absorbed in work that you love or conversing with somebody whose company you enjoy with openness and independence, will lead to your happiness. This doesn't come from seeking popularity, appreciation or praise.

For a short book (184 pages), this certainly has many concepts worth reading at least twice. You probably get more from this book on the second reading (I know I did), and hopefully, you will receive some happiness from this. The actual book is far more interesting than what I have written here. Anthony De Mello combines stories with all of these ideas, making this very easy reading. If you like what I have written, do yourself a big favour and buy the book. It certainly changed me for the better, and I can only hope it does the same for you.

CHAPTER FOURTEEN

The Power of Your Subconscious Mind (Joseph Murphy 1963)

Joseph Murphy was born a catholic in Ireland in 1898, and he moved to the US in the 1920s. He spent a large proportion of his life questioning organised religion and developing a new way of thinking about life and obtaining goals. He also spent time in India studying non-Christian religions.

The Power of Your Subconscious Mind is probably his best-known and most popular work exploring the notion that your thoughts control your destiny. As we think, feel and believe "things", this affects the condition of our minds and our body, which in turn changes our immediate environment. The law of life is the law of our beliefs.

We all know how strong a magnet is, and a magnetised person is full of confidence and faith. They "know" that they will win. Whereas a de-magnetised person is full of fear and doubt, which prevents them from going forward in life. This is where the power of the subconscious can change everything; it can deliver everything to you that you desire as long as you are open-minded and receptive.

The law of your mind is the law of belief - you just have to believe. Whatever you experience in life is the reaction of your subconscious mind to your thoughts. The belief is what brings about the results. Stop believing in doubts, opinions, and fear. Instead, fill your mind with harmony, health, peace, goodwill, and amazing things will happen in your life.

Your mind has two parts, the conscious and the unconscious. Your subconscious mind is a reflection of your habitual thinking. Whatever you are thinking affects much of what happens to your body and the environment, so thoughts of peace, happiness and prosperity will deliver only positive outcomes. When we can control our thoughts properly, then the power of the subconscious becomes our greatest tool. If you want to change the external conditions in your life, you must change how you are using your subconscious. Most of us try to change the external first, which doesn't work. Most of our greatest challenges are within us.

Conversely, when we have thoughts of fear, anger and anxiety, which are all negative, the mind holds a sense of panic and despair. By speaking firmly, we can prevent this.

The subconscious takes everything we say at face value. If you say, "I can't afford it, "your subconscious is provoked to see that you cannot buy it. The subconscious will know that you can buy it by reversing that statement immediately. This means we have to be careful in how we say things. Remember that the law of life is the law of belief, and a belief is a thought in your mind. Think positive and be positive with what you say, and you can improve your future.

Our conscious is the reasoning part of our mind that we make all of our decisions with it. Once our subconscious accepts any idea, it begins to use that idea. If we believe something, our subconscious merely accepts this and won't argue with it. The subconscious doesn't know the difference between right and wrong - it just assumes that everything from the conscious is true.

Our conscious mind's "job" is to protect the sub from negativity, acting as a little gatekeeper to the sub-conscious. If we believe in the fears and the opinions of others, then the fear will bring negativity.

However, this will only happen if we accept this as being true. When we feel negative about something, the power of auto-suggestion can turn things around. We can overcome the negative situation by saying positive statements, believing in them, and repeating them several times.

People can restore their memory and overcome a nasty temper by practicing auto-suggestions in reverse. Suggestions can be both constructive and destructive; it is really up to us which one we use. As children, most of us have heard negative suggestions such as "you haven't got a chance" or "you'll never amount to anything." These things were only said to control us and put fear into us as kids. As adults, it is up to us to change our thoughts about these comments to give us more positivity in our lives.

When you think about it, much of society works this way, which is why many of us have unrealised dreams. Whatever the suggestions are of others, we have our thoughts, and we can choose the positives of life, love and health. Remember to think of beauty, peace and abundance and to know that these things are yours if you believe them. It sounds fairly simple, doesn't it? But ask yourself how often negativity has been a part of your life in the last month. We need to be aware of how we are thinking.

Negativity can be found everywhere if you want to see it. "The economy stinks", "I am too old to learn", or "I don't know the right people." These are just negative thoughts which bring about lack, limitation and frustrations in your life. You will always find people (if you want to) that will say and believe this. This thinking, if continued, can lead to sickness and mental disorders. Don't "buy" into it. Instead, relax and let go of these thoughts and replace them with positivity and see the difference it makes for yourself.

Chapter 3 deals with the "Miracle-working Power of Your

Subconscious." Simply put, you can discover this by stating to your subconscious before going to sleep a task you want to do and then letting the power of your brain go to work. Murphy says, "what you write on the inside, you will experience on the outside," which is true. We are always writing our book of life as we go - which way we want to go is up to us. Much of the pain and misery in the world comes from us not understanding this. We are at our best when we are in peace, harmony and divine order. Our beliefs can then cure many of the ills that we experience. Imagine a happy ending or solution to any issue you face and feel the enjoyment. What we imagine and feel will be worked on by our subconscious.

Throughout history, there have been countless examples of healers working their magic through the power of suggestion and acceptance. Those healers would have talked as though the healing had already been completed at the start, thus affecting the person's mind needing healing. The Bible is full of phrases that are similar in thinking to this. Whether or not you are religious, these phrases in Chapter 4 are very powerful. Jesus insists throughout the Bible that faith (or planting a seed) is the way forward in manifesting your thoughts. Jesus healed through the power of faith and the healing power of the subconscious mind.

Healing by hypnosis works from the power of suggestion, an open mind, and the subconscious power. Other forms of healing work in similar ways, but the primary healing process is having faith in a positive outcome that works by using the power of the subconscious mind.

Modern day healing (chapter 5) works in similar ways. A healer removes the physical block by their actions, enabling the healing currents to work. None of our modern practitioners claim that they 'healed' the patient. The most important thing to realise is to imagine the end result and feel how real it is. The infinite life principle will respond to your conscious and your request. In other words, believe that you have received, and then you shall receive. "If thou canst believe, all things are possible to him that believeth" Mark 9:23. In much the same way, the power of prayer works. In fact, any method, which moves you from fear and worries to faith and expectancy, will heal. Anything from Voodoo to magnets can be successful.

Thinking of harmony and pure health can restore through the kinetic action of the subconscious while we sleep. Stop thinking about ailments, and they will be cut off from your body. Think and talk about being healthy regularly, and this is what you will experience.

First, we need a mental image in our mind before the subconscious can work its "magic." There are many ways of doing processes in life; there are also techniques for having your prayers answered. Your prayers should aim to accomplish something rather than being a random thought. As with the blueprint to your house, you have a mental home and a blueprint for happiness and abundance. We build on this all the time as our thoughts and mental imagery create our blueprint. We must build silently by having peace, harmony, joy and goodwill in the present moment.

There are nine techniques to use, and they are:

1. Visualisation technique
2. Mental movie method
3. The Baudoin technique
4. Sleeping technique
5. Thank-you technique
6. Affirmative method
7. The Argumentative method
8. Absolute method
9. The Decree method

Read the book and discover the best method for yourself. As 90% of our mental life is subconscious, those who fail to use it properly don't achieve what we are capable of. Our subconscious always tells us to grow, advance, transcend and move forward to greater heights.

Our conscious mind can interfere with our health by believing in others' false beliefs, fears, and opinions. When this happens, the subconscious mind has no other option than to act on it. The subconscious mind has a life of its own, moving towards happiness, positivity and good health. We need to be in harmony with the universe for this to happen.

Remember, we are the sum of all of our thoughts. As a result, we must substitute negative thoughts for positive ones, and then the "bad" will disappear. When we feel negative, start your counteraction force of affirmations, and the benefits will show.

The main reasons for lack of success are putting in too much effort and having no confidence. When your subconscious accepts any idea, it begins to execute it. Your positive thoughts can lead to the answer you want, and negative thoughts do the opposite. Using your willpower won't be as effective as the subconscious doesn't respond well to being told what to do. The subconscious requires positive feelings and thoughts to respond well. Forcing something to happen never ends well here and is like trying to force a square peg into a round hole. Forcing anything in general rarely works, but many of us still try to do things this way. Your imagination works wonders on your mind to show you where to go. Imagine the problem/situation has already resolved itself, and success will follow.

Have you ever tried using force to remember something? It rarely works. Trying to force things to happen (e.g., getting a good result in an exam) usually results in the opposite of what you asked for.

Use your imagination, mainly just before you go to sleep, to paint a picture of the desired outcome.

With finances, we need to convince our minds that we will always be in abundance, never just trying to make ends meet. Always do what you love and feel passionate about; never just do a job because it pays well. Wealth and success go well together, and we have to have positive feelings about both. The feelings are important; instead of just saying "I am wealthy" and not meaning it, the feelings are what our subconscious accepts to be true. Say, "I am wealthy", and feel you are wealthy. Make your affirmations about wealth and success before you go to bed, and be careful of your language. Anything that involves lack or limitation will bring those values into your life. Remember, fear brings everything down. Any negative thoughts about yourself or others pull away success/wealth and bring about the opposite. By being on good mental terms with everyone in your life, you are open to the possibility of the positive results that you want.

We live in an abundant world, so each of us can be rich, happy and free. There is no need to fight over "things," we just need to allow abundance to happen. Having wealth means we can do what we want and never not do something because of a lack. The hoarding of money (which is fear) doesn't achieve happiness of any kind. Instead, feel as though money flows freely in your life and that there is always abundance.

Another reason for lack of wealth is that many people are either condemning openly through spoken words or silently through thoughts. Some people feel some form of virtuosi with poverty, but the reality is there is no virtue in this. Conversely, a love of money brings riches. The most important thing to do is think positively about yourself and those around you and be careful about what you say to achieve what you want. As with all things positive, if we can imagine being wealthy, being healthy, and achieving our goals, then the subconscious will do what is necessary to achieve that.

Success involves three basic steps:

1. Find out what you love to do - then do it. Love your work.
2. Specialise in some particular type of work and know it better than anyone else.
3. Your desire must not be selfish and must benefit humanity.

Remember, there is no success without peace of mind, and we create what we believe - if you take nothing else from this book, remember this. When we are successful, we love our work. Sometimes we need to be actors – acting as though we are successful to achieve that outcome. At any age, we can learn this, but obviously, the younger, the better.

When buying and selling, our conscious mind is the starter, and the subconscious is the motor. The first step is to quieten down, relax and be at peace, and meditation helps here. The second step is to imagine what your desired outcome is - trusting the process of your deeper mind. There are many ways your prayers may be answered - "as within, so without." Go to sleep feeling and believing that you are successful and perfectly satisfied. You will eventually succeed in growing the idea of success into your deeper mind.

Many of our most famous scientists have used their subconscious minds to achieve great advances. By using the power of imagination and building from this, complex "problems" were solved. The important thing here is to relax, get quiet and let the subconscious do its magic. No pushing or rushing here is critical to show some patience. The answers don't always come overnight. Believe that you have the answer before going to sleep and have faith that the outcome will be achieved. Joseph

Murphy recalls many interesting stories in the book that show this process working. Read these when you buy his book. Before sleeping, ask what you want – what do you have to lose?

Restful sleep is essential in our healing processes and finding our answers in life. These may be the main reasons why we sleep. As we sleep, our subconscious mind is always working. Prayer can be valuable here as a lack of sleep disturbs these processes. People who 'survive' on less than 6 hours of sleep per day are making everything harder for themselves. Have you ever woken up in the middle of the night with a 'fantastic' idea only to forget it by the morning?

Chapter 14 refers to relationships. One of the most important concepts here is to realise that your partner isn't responsible for your health, wealth, love or happiness. That is your job. Thinking that these things will automatically happen by living with someone else is fanciful. The idea of changing your partner into something you want rarely works. The "ideal" couple shares these things with mutual love and respect. Forgiveness, gratitude, and not taking anyone for granted create strong, healthy relationships.

Happiness is a choice of mind - so just be happy. Happiness can come from external things (e.g., having a child), but these events don't provide lasting happiness. We can choose to feel and be it – sounds strange and simple, doesn't it? Most of the best things in life are simple. Make it a habit to be happy because being happy is a habit. Imagine you are a spiritual magnet that attracts health, prosperity and happiness. We must sincerely desire to be happy - many people, however, seem to enjoy being miserable and sad (a bit like Eeyore from the stories of Pooh). Why do people do this? It's because of their habits of having negative beliefs, such as "I can't do that" or "it's all right for you to say that." Our lives are what we make of them, and happiness is mental and spiritual. Some people say, "I would be happy if I had a million dollars", but that won't bring lasting happiness. This is because happiness comes from within us, not from external sources. If this weren't the case, then all billionaires would be happy.

From the Bible (Matthew), "think of others how you would want them to think of you." Likewise with your feelings. Negative thoughts can be quite destructive to us. If we cheat and deceive others, we are cheating and deceiving ourselves. How we think, feel and act towards others boomerangs back to us. Many of us get "involved" in the media and social media with our beliefs and react negatively. There is a lot to be said for limiting our exposure to these forms of media while realising that we can disagree with others. We can do so with an open heart (no anger). Our annoyance with people may be due to some subconscious pattern or mental projection from us. In other words, we cause our own annoyance. How we react to things in life is our choice.

"I am not my thoughts; I am the thinker of my thoughts" - Jim Fortin.

When you damage someone's ego, you cannot gain their goodwill as everyone wants to be loved and appreciated. Instead of "winning" an argument, make the other person feel important, and goodwill will follow. The problem for most of us (especially myself) is that we want to show how intelligent we all are. The reality is that "really intelligent" people just don't need to do this. This is not to say that you let people walk all over you with their temper or through bullying; instead, be firm in your beliefs and respectful of others. It is okay not to back down; how you do it will gain others' respect.

God/universe (whichever you believe in) has nothing to do with the chaos in the world - we bring that on ourselves by negative and destructive thinking. If we think about harmony with nature, then our life force will deliver our health, harmony, and peace. Negative thoughts stop this. Remember, "to err is human, but forgiveness (of others and yourself) is divine." Criticism can only hurt us if we allow it to – so why do it? We just need to master our thoughts, reactions and emotions! Once we can do this, we can truly and honestly forgive people for any sins.

As with all problems, the solution lies inside the situation. The subconscious has the answers; we just have to let it work. The subconscious can automatically take over by having positive habits and building tracks in your mind. Good habits are so powerful. The only obstacles to healing/happiness are our own thoughts. To achieve our desires, we must first relax our bodies and get into a meditative state. Then we can switch our imagination to what we want to achieve.

You are halfway there already whenever you have a destructive habit that you want to get rid of. The process is easy to accomplish when your desire to get rid of a habit is stronger than the actual habit. Whenever we use our emotions for this, the subconscious will rid us of the pattern. Destructive habits like alcoholism and excessive smoking come from negative and destructive thinking. The magic steps for freedom here are outlined on page 128. When you read the book yourself, you will discover the power of these steps.

Fear is probably man's greatest enemy, and it causes sickness, failure and conflicts. The crazy thing is that fear is just a thought in your mind, meaning that you have become afraid of your thoughts. It sounds a little silly, doesn't it? To overcome fear, we must do what we are afraid to do. If fear of heights is your thing, challenge yourself to do something like abseiling down a cliff. This was one of my fears, and doing this was far easier to do than I thought it would be. Fear of failure holds many of us back from achieving what we would like to do. One technique for overcoming fear is to get quiet for 5-10 minutes and visualise what you are fearful of. If repeated, this can be imprinted on your subconscious, and the problem will be less troublesome. A fear of falling and noise were given to us as a form of self-protection at birth. All other fears come from our environment and our early influencers in life. Our imagination can cause abnormal fears, which can manifest in reality - or our perceived reality. Abnormal fears disappear by moving your attention to something that you would rather think about. Being at peace and using meditation help with all of this.

Our subconscious mind never tires or grows old. For those who can hold onto positive values you will always remain young in spirit. All of us have seen people whose demeanour is much younger than their actual age. This is important as the fear of time causes many of us to age prematurely. We never need to grow old in our thoughts, and it is said that "age is not the flight of years, but the dawn of wisdom." You can enjoy telling your kids this. Enjoy the passing of years as what we call death is really just another journey to a new dimension of life. We are what we think; therefore, you are as young as you think you are. Don't use words like retired, old or finished when describing yourself.

Also, we are as strong as we believe and as valuable as we think we are. Some people are old at thirty, whilst others are young at eighty. Our minds and our thoughts determine who we are. Age combined with strong positive thoughts over a long time can be invaluable in many positions. People over sixty-five shouldn't be asked to resign. Instead, they should be encouraged to help make decisions and guide others based on their experience. Do you think Warren Buffett and Charlie Munger believe they are old and obsolete? Our minds can keep us young. Never think of yourself as old as your mind never retires - so why should you? Retirement can just mean a new venture. The main difference for most is that instead of making a living, we can focus on living life to its fullest. Think of yourself as happy, radiant, successful and powerful.

This inspiring book teaches about our unconscious mind and how powerful it is in determining the paths that we take in life. So much of ourselves comes from our thoughts and determines our path in life. For those who have read this book, reread it, as there are probably little 'gems' that you have missed. For those who haven't, buy the book and read it; your mind can make life so much better for you.

CHAPTER FIFTEEN

Dollars Flow to Me Easily (Richard Dotts) 2015

Who is Richard Dotts? From reading this book and looking at his other books, it is safe to say that he is very spiritual and believes, as I do, in the abundance that there is in our world. Richard's message that all changes can be easy if you allow them to be is important. Practice putting your trust in the universe. Achieving financial freedom seems to be the goal for most of us. Some find it easy, while some will never reach that place of freedom. This book is about making it easier.

Unfortunately, we have all been conditioned by our parents (meaning well) and society to believe that making money is difficult and that it is bad to have too much (whatever too much actually is, it is just another story that we can decide to make or not). So much of this programming ties us down and affects our higher vibration, which is required to accumulate money. These negative thoughts can make it very difficult to manifest money as they create obstacles on the way to financial freedom.

There are two ways in which people get stuck with living. The first is the belief that to change; things must be difficult. Everything in modern day living and our expectations around those things negatively affects our vibrations, which in turn affects our outcome negatively. The second way is to continue to focus on what the problem is. Overanalysing things in our minds make financial problems appear worse than they are. Once we understand this, life then becomes easier. Sometimes the best way to solve a problem is to stop thinking about it and think about something else entirely different.

When there is a recurring negative pattern in your life, it shows an unconscious/subconscious belief that you are holding onto that isn't helping you. An example would be if you work in retail and are constantly thinking that the poor economy is why you are not doing well. However, the reality of this belief is that there are always opportunities to do well regardless of the economy. The underlying pattern is the root of the problem that causes you to think, feel, and react in a certain way, repeatedly strengthening the belief. We don't realise that we are doing this most of the time. As the author says, read this book with your heart rather than your head, and you will get more out of it. In other words, don't overthink.

Think of your mind as a transmitter and a receiver of frequencies you are conscious of. When information 'pops' into your mind and you become aware of it, understand that this has come from the universe. It sounds a little woo-woo, doesn't it, but when you are at peace with your surroundings, you will be open to the information coming through.

You won't receive the whole message of this book by reading what I have written here. If you are reading this without reading the entire book, you miss the whole point. The author is trying to change and transform your thinking – to remove your resistance to money.

Chapter 2 explores feelings, becoming aware of our surroundings and acknowledging the abundance around us. Also, letting go of ego and clearing your mind of the senseless "monkey chatter'" which is going on inside. Mindless "monkey chatter" includes reaction to "stuff" you see through social media, TV programs, partisan politics, and so-called facts that are really opinions. Most of this "stuff" doesn't help us individually, but we still do it. We then take this and make it mean much more than it actually does.

Chapter 3 looks at staying connected with the universe, appreciating what is around us, and ridding ourselves of perceptions of money issues and problems that we THINK we have. Our thoughts can certainly make life difficult for us! Looking back to our past is not helpful as it drains us of positive energy (we don't drive our cars by looking in the rear-view mirror all of the time). We must stay in the present and think about money, abundance and prosperity in all aspects of our life. Good things will happen by dropping the negative feelings of worry and fear.

We have to focus on our inner feelings of abundance for most of our day instead of focusing on external influences. Your bank balance is a prime example. This is not easy to do as we have conditioned ourselves for years to think that our net worth equals our self-worth, which never brings any long-term happiness.

Self-judgment doesn't help us with abundance feelings either. Our brains will fight this as it tries to solve 'problems' with practical solutions. This is similar to when a wife goes to a husband (partner or whatever) with a problem. She really wants her partner to listen and show empathy, but the husband usually tries to "fix" things instead. The reality is that we have to be aware of our thoughts and feelings ALL of the time. The author details this and gives examples to explain this more clearly.

In a book that is seemingly about "dollars", you will notice that very little is written about actually making money. For most of us, our well-being is directly linked to our finances. Western society has taught us many things, but this isn't one of them. Most of our issues relating to money are self-created problems. We tend to focus on a lack of money (scarcity mindset), which pushes opportunities away. Therefore this manifests scarcity and "confirms" our beliefs that money isn't abundant. Instead, we are told to be practical (whatever that means) and hold onto money; otherwise, we will lose it. Think about how this is true. The continued worry about how much money we have has a negative effect. It causes our worries to become our reality.

If you need to know your financial situation, don't dwell on it for more than fifteen minutes a day. Once you get used to fifteen minutes, it is easy to reduce it to zero minutes. The more we focus on our lack of finances, the more worried we become. Where does worry usually get you? Nowhere. Negative feelings go hand in hand with worry, and both act against you attracting wealth.

The feelings we hold are the key, not the actual things we worry about. Once we can control our feelings and thoughts, then more opportunities arise. As we realise that most things are possible, all we need is to focus on our end goal for a period of time and leave everything else to the universe. When creating your own goal, be very specific about what you want, as the universe doesn't understand vague thoughts. A lack of belief can be destructive to our goals. We need to stop focusing on the lack of success or wealth and focus on abundance everywhere to attract abundance.

Like most things in life, these changes don't happen immediately, but there will be a positive shift sooner than you think by feeling good and being at peace. Manifestations of wealth are not about trying to make things happen on the outside; it is more about awareness of abundance and the natural flow of things.

When we don't like our present situation, this is because of our outer projection. Our outer projection is how we perceive the world, whereas our inner state is how we think and feel about ourselves. We have to change our inner state first and free it from worry to change this.

The title of chapter 6 (How to manifest money and abundance in your life) makes it the most popular chapter, but without the foundation provided by the rest of the book, it is ineffective. It's an important chapter to read for yourself, and you will discover this when you buy the book.

The next chapter is about how the universe stores all of our positive thoughts and aspirations. However, it also stores the negative ones. Your vibrations play a key role here as being able to receive will not occur while your vibrations, or energy, are the opposite of positive. There is an exercise about sitting quietly by yourself which is very powerful. Ultimately, the aim is to drop your previous baggage, become aware of the good in you and let go of your negative beliefs. Another important concept here is self-love – as we have to love and believe in ourselves first before anything else. Receiving from the universe isn't greed - it is merely the recognition of what you ask for.

Letting go of our negative thoughts isn't easy at first, as our ego mind will want to drag us back into the "reality" of life. Ego wants you to plan for the future to keep you "safe", and although this sounds practical, it doesn't work in the same way as the universe does. Instead, shift your focus to your inner self, live your life in the now (i.e., enjoy today) and rid yourself of all the negatives you have held in your lifetime.

Chapter 8 deals with giving up any need to try to be abundant. It is important, as trying to get something causes worry, which causes the opposite. Remember, worry can never help us achieve our goals and why it is important not to focus on our bank balances. We need to let go of our negative thoughts. The hard part about this is changing our thoughts, which we have held for so long. But never force things to happen. Just close your eyes, keep turning your focus inside yourself and let go of the negatives. As with all things practicing helps here.

The best part is that letting go of fear, worry, disappointment, and frustration makes you feel good, opening opportunities.

As we turn our attention to the good feelings of joy and peace, we find our lives more fulfilled, and the title "Dollars flow to me easily" becomes more apparent. As we feel this way, we find that other people's behaviour and external things have little or no influence over us. Other techniques, like manifestation, can work for shorter periods but rarely last as long.

Living in the now and focusing on our inner state is crucial. Get away from thinking that financial good comes from external sources and get used to feeling the good inside you. We all have this ability, and you will be amazed at the results when you become this way.

Chapter 10 looks at your journey having been finished, and even though it is quite short, it is so powerful. You will find out yourself when you read it.

This is one of a selection of books by Richard Dotts that inform us of the power of peace and spirituality. This book is another that Jim Fortin introduced to me.

Well worth reading at least a couple of times to discover that really, "Dollars flow to me easily." You have to find out for yourself what path you want to take.

Epilogue

You have read the book – so what is next?

My personal recommendation is to buy and read the fifteen books that I have discussed in this book. Some people may feel that they want to read a couple of these. But, that may not be what you feel is best for you. We all come from different backgrounds, and what is right for some won't be right for others. Whatever you do is up to you.

The worst thing that you can do is read this book, say, "that was interesting", then just put it on a shelf, or close the kindle app, and go about life without applying any of the knowledge. Reading is great, I wish more people did it, but reading alone WON'T transform you. Applying the ideas in this book will be how your life can become easier and happier. Do the exercises in the recommended books, and for the books that don't have exercises (such as Ms Shinn's work), write your own notes and go over these daily.

Our habits are what can make life easy or harder; the choice is ours. Please make it a habit of being grateful for the things in your life. Smile at yourself and smile at others (it isn't that hard), and you will discover that people will smile back. Love yourself and tell yourself how awesome you are. Do this, and you are going to be happy in life.

The world is beautiful; make the most of your life and enjoy it.

Contact the Author

Facebook "Money Does Grow on Trees – 15 Books that can change your life" **https://www.facebook.com/Money-Does-Grow-on-Trees-15-Books-that-can-change-your-life-111078394908903**

Email **johnbolton981@gmail.com**